Cambridge Elements ≡

Elements in Corporate Governance
edited by
Thomas Clarke
UTS Business School, University of Technology Sydney

VALUE-CREATING BOARDS

Challenges for Future Research and Practice

Morten Huse
BI Norwegian Business School

CAMBRIDGE
UNIVERSITY PRESS

CAMBRIDGE
UNIVERSITY PRESS

University Printing House, Cambridge CB2 8BS, United Kingdom

One Liberty Plaza, 20th Floor, New York, NY 10006, USA

477 Williamstown Road, Port Melbourne, VIC 3207, Australia

314–321, 3rd Floor, Plot 3, Splendor Forum, Jasola District Centre,
New Delhi – 110025, India

79 Anson Road, #06–04/06, Singapore 079906

Cambridge University Press is part of the University of Cambridge.

It furthers the University's mission by disseminating knowledge in the pursuit of
education, learning, and research at the highest international levels of excellence.

www.cambridge.org
Information on this title: www.cambridge.org/9781108463911
DOI: 10.1017/9781108564786

© Morten Huse 2018

First published 2018

A catalogue record for this publication is available from the British Library.

ISBN 978-1-108-46391-1 Paperback
ISSN 2515-7175 (online)
ISSN 2515-7167 (print)

Value-Creating Boards

Morten Huse

Abstract: *This Element shapes the discussion about corporate governance and boards of directors. The arena for boards and corporate governance is not static.* In Boards, Governance and Value Creation *(Cambridge 2007), Morten Huse presented knowledge about boards with a focus on behavioural perspectives. The present contribution reflects on what has occurred during recent years. It contributes to the literature around sustainable value creation in business and society. This Element brings an update of the content of the 2007 book and thus provides a resource for students and scholars – as well as for reflective practitioners.*

Keywords: *boards of directors, value creation, research stream, future, behaviour*

Issns: *2515-7175 (online) 2515-7167 (print)*

Isbns: *9781108463911 (PB) 9781108564786 (OC)*

1 Introduction

What is behind concepts such as 'value-creating boards' and 'board governance'? Both concepts are increasingly being used.[1] My previous book, *Boards, Governance and Value Creation: The Human Side of Corporate Governance* (BGV; Huse 2007), has

---

[1] See e.g. Kehoe, Lund & Spielmann (2016), McKinsey & Company (www .mckinsey.com/business-functions/strategy-and-corporate-finance/our-insights/toward-a-value-creating-board) downloaded February 2017. See also training programmes for board members at e.g. IESE, INSEAD, Wharton, NACD, Board Performance Group. Major auditing companies such as Deloitte, PWC and KPMG also use these concepts.

contributed to the development of these concepts. I have been asked several times to publish a revised version of *Boards, Governance and Value Creation.*[2] The book appeared on the market ten years ago, and there is now a need for revisiting some of its teachings. My objective with *Value-Creating Boards* is to update the content of the 2007 book and thus provide a contemporary resource for students of corporate governance – as well as for reflective practitioners. The overall objective is to continue shaping the discussion about corporate governance and boards of directors, but it is not a straightforward project to write a book about boards of directors for an international audience.[3] Boards and corporate governance systems vary across countries. However, I have some freedom in that my academic training is in a US tradition, I am living in Scandinavia, and I have experiences from universities and businesses in several countries.

BGV has received attention around the world and from many different audiences. Students, faculty and practitioners from all over the world frequently contact me and tell me that this book was a building block for their PhD research or practice. Researchers and professors present it as the cornerstone in

---

[2] I am writing this Element in an informal way, and it reflects what I have been learning. I thus often write 'I' or 'mine'. However, I am working and have been working with a large number of scholars and friends. Sometimes it may be difficult to distinguish between what I have done and what we have done together. Research usually goes through many phases and is much more than the published products. It can thus also be difficult to identify the contributions of each person. I present what has been learned from each and everyone. In the text, I will also frequently use 'we' and 'our'. This will reflect that some of us have been working together on this issue. It will, however, also sometimes include the readers in the presentations.

[3] The use of the term 'boards of directors' is not straightforward when making international comparisons. The term's background comes from an Anglo-American understanding. This is evidenced, for example, when making comparisons across various national corporate governance codes. Other terms found in various codes include 'boards of executives', 'boards of supervisors', 'boards of managers', 'boards of representatives', 'board of auditors' or just 'boards'. The charges of the various boards may be different but also overlapping. However, I have decided to use the terms 'boards' and 'boards of directors', as it may be too complicated to use numerous terms.

a developing stream of research, and businesses and policymakers develop their agendas based on it. The book attracted a lot of attention: in 2008 I was invited to present it to the leadership and major customers of the Bank of Thailand. BGV was also recommended in the newsletter of a US association of optometrists, and it was reviewed and recommended as recently as 2015 in *El Mercurio*, a leading business newspaper in Latin America.

The arena for boards and corporate governance has not been static during the past decade, and developments have actually escalated. In BGV, I attempted to accumulate knowledge about boards of directors with a focus on behavioural perspectives. In this Element, I will reflect on what has been happening since 2007. Whether we like it or not, research is loaded with values, and with this Element I want to contribute to sustainable value creation in business and society. The presentation is not unbiased, as I view the debates through the lens of an internationally based management scholar, and my focus is on strategy, organization and leadership. That does not mean that I fail to acknowledge contributions from those using other lenses, but we should all be aware of an author's perspective when reading a book.

1.1   Building on Previous Contributions

Although considerable attention today is given to boards, value creation and behavioural perspectives of corporate governance, the majority of studies about boards and value creation are still applying input/output approaches without giving attention to processes and the human side. Most studies are still focusing on only a few explanatory or predictive variables such as the number of board members, insider/outsider ratio, CEO duality and the share holdings of the board members. These are often given the 'usual suspect' label (Finkelstein & Mooney 2003). More recently, the number of women on boards has also been a popular variable or measure in research. The dependent performance variable is still often a measure of corporate financial performance, but measures about societal performance are also becoming popular.

We need to go beyond the usual suspects. Our focus should not only be on the easy-to-place pieces in a complicated jigsaw. The most important and interesting pictures may be displayed only when we are able to place the more difficult ones. Furthermore, it is important not to start from scratch every time we begin our explorations. We need to understand where we are, and then go further. We need to build on what we know and then, based on the accumulation of knowledge, go into what we do not know (Daily, Dalton & Cannella 2003).

We should challenge borders in topics, methods and theories. We need to approach important and unexplored issues, and not only make sophisticated replications of what we already know. Within an input-process–output-context approach, my contribution has largely been to go deeper into behavioural perspectives. This includes the use of methods that help us understand actors, their motivations and their interactions. It also includes the use of holistic approaches where behaviour, context and time are important factors.

Before presenting the six challenges for value-creating boards that I want to bring attention to, I will present research on these topics since BGV's publication. I will particularly focus on research and studies I have been involved in but also relate this work to the contributions of others. I want to be explorative and help 'dismantle fortresses' (Daily et al. 2003) and challenge borders of existing knowledge and research. Such explorative research may need to be adventurous and does not always fit into traditional methods of deduction.

An update of recent research and studies about value-creating boards is presented in Section 2.

1.2   *Factors of Value-Creating Boards: Challenging Borders*

I will go further in this Element than I have in the past. I will present six sets of factors that should be building blocks for how we meet future challenges for researching and developing boards of directors. They all contribute to the understanding of value-creating boards. The six sets of factors are shaped by lessons learnt from recent corporate governance events, the development of various megatrends, recent research and my own private and professional experiences.

1.2.1 Theorizing about Value-Creating Boards

The first factor is the development of the extended team production approach and theorizing about value-creating boards. Attempts are being made to introduce a grand theory of corporate governance.[4] Agency theory has been the corporate governance bible for some decades. Agency theory is built on certain easy-to-communicate and often simplistic assumptions. I have been reflecting on an alternative grand theory of corporate governance. The efforts have been towards developing a theory wherein macro meets micro, and where negative consequences of the present corporate governance picture can be overcome or addressed. BGV introduced factors that could be seen as initial steps for an alternative grand theory, and since the BGV publication in 2007, I have been triggered by the potential of an extended team production approach. However, when including behavioural perspectives, approaches to a grand theory should be downplayed, as we need our predictions to focus on contingency perspectives and importance of the context.

Team production theory (Blair 1995; Blair & Stout 1999) has been mentioned as an alternative to agency theory. The first factor of value-creating boards is the development of an extended version of team production theory. Team production theory acknowledges the importance of context and contingencies. The extended version also pushes behavioural perspectives and opens the door for integrating Blair's (1995) version of team production theory with the leadership and team development literature. The extended team production theory and the challenge of theorizing are presented in Factor 1 (Section 3.1).

---

[4] Examples include the initiatives by William Judge and the establishment of the International Corporate Governance Society.

1.2.2   Boards Should Be Involved Where They
Add the Most Value

The second factor is that boards should contribute to shared value creation and be involved where they add the most value. Value creation is the dependent variable in most of my arguments. BGV paved the way for me to get to know people developing business practices and effective boards of directors.[5] Through these people, I received hands-on knowledge and experience about how to develop boards and board members. I present this factor as the product of lessons learnt from approaching the business community about value creation.

Value may sometimes be difficult to communicate and measure. A core concept is sustained or long-term sustainable value, but value should also be identified and measured in intermediate steps: e.g. the value creation by individual board members and other actors, value creation of board processes and procedures, board-level value creation, firm-level value creation and the value created for the society and other stakeholders.

I identify myself as a scholar in entrepreneurship and strategy. Through business community interactions, I found that a value-chain approach was highly appreciated. Another input from recent resource approaches to strategy includes concepts such as 'absorptive capacity', 'dynamic capabilities' and 'ambidexterity'. Definitions of value creation and the boards' contribution to value creation are presented in Factor 2 (Section 3.2).

1.2.3   Preparing for the Future and the Digital
Transformation of Society.

Megatrends include the digital transformation of society; the focus on equity and gender equality in society, business and on corporate boards; migration and inclusion; and globalization and the knowledge society. Digitalization was one of the issues I hardly discussed in BGV. The third factor, then, concerns the

---

[5] In particular, Randi Ib in Denmark (www.board-governance.com) and Tracy Long in the UK (www.boardroomreview.com).

consequences of the digital transformation of society. These consequences are far reaching and may completely change the present corporate picture. Moreover, its speed is escalating. We may within a few years experience a complete paradigm shift relevant to value-creating boards.

The main factors for developing value-creating boards must include perspectives relating to the future. For me, important events during the recent decade include the introduction of the Norwegian legislation securing gender balance on corporate boards, the financial crisis in 2008–2009, the corporate pay gap, the election of Donald Trump as president of the United States, anti-corruption initiatives and the consequences of the Panama and Paradise paper explorations. Preparing for the future and the digital transformation of society are presented in Factor 3 (Section 3.3).

1.2.4 Going beyond the Surface: Understanding Actors and Dynamics

Among the core contributions from BGV were the emphases on micro-level approaches and on understanding the human side of boards and governance. The fourth factor goes deeper into the micro level and focuses on micro-level issues that are important for boards, governance and value creation.

Attention needs to be directed to the dynamics stemming from actors, their motivations and their interactions. Lessons from sociology and psychology, can support us in our explorations. We need to understand identities, social identities and identification of core actors. We can learn more about the types of capital they have, and about their career and work/life preferences. In this factor, I present findings from my recent research and my interest in micro-level issues. A major lesson is that individuals can make changes. Individual actors can have a profound impact on value creation for business and society.

I have used this emphasis in my recent empirical research effort focused on getting more women on boards. I used a micro-level approach (mentoring advocates) to understand how individual actors might contribute to influencing boards regarding gender equality and public policies. That research provided insights into the identities, motivations and preferences of core actors. Understanding actors and dynamics is presented in Factor 4 (Section 3.4)

1.2.5   Diversity and Women on Boards: The Business Case

Research related to women on corporate boards has recently in general been mushrooming. Women's contributions to boards have for many years been one of my core research interests. However, I find most of the present publications on the topic uninspiring, and studies about the business case for women on boards are often based on insufficient or even incorrect assumptions. The attention to individual actors and the human side is missing. In addition, the majority of this research does not build on knowledge about value-creating boards and actual board behaviour. In the fifth factor (Section 3.5), I present five points as input to an alternative business case for women on boards, and I lean on the framework from BGV.

1.2.6   When Micro Meets Macro: Contributing in Actual Discourses

The introduction of a gender quota on corporate boards in Norway opened the doors for women to parliaments, politics and public policymaking in several countries. As Factor 6, I present the snowball that started rolling in Norway – about getting women on boards (Machold et al. 2013). The international landscape about the presence and recruitment of women on boards has completely changed since 2007. Such changes may have far-reaching consequences for business and society. The direction and consequences of the snowball may be variable in the beginning, but if these consequences are not properly heeded, then tremendous damages from a potential avalanche may occur. Factor 6 (Section 3.6) reminds us about our responsibility to actively contribute to ongoing discourses.

1.3 The Development of a Research Stream

Since 1990, my agenda has included developing research about behavioural perspectives of boards and governance. The Norefjell Board Governance International Research workshops on behavioural perspective on boards of directors have been crucial for developing and disseminating research and knowledge about actual board behaviour.[6] During the fourteen years (2004–2017) with the Norefjell workshops in the Norwegian mountains, this group of behavioural governance researchers has discussed and explored ways to research and understand behavioural perspectives of boards of directors. These workshops have been the cornerstone in the development of a distinct international research stream about boards of directors (Gabrielsson et al. 2014; Huse 2009a). The stream is rooted in possibilities and challenges in European research communities, as well in European business and politics. The importance of publishing in US-based journals is acknowledged, but this needs to be balanced with doing meaningful and impactful research. The building blocks and direction of this research stream about value-creating boards were summarized in Huse (2009a) in *Value Creating Boards: Corporate Governance and Organizational Behaviour* (VCB). I will present this research stream in the final section (Section 4), where I present my current research agenda.

2 Building on Previous Contributions

In the past decade, considerable academic attention has focused on boards, governance and value creation, and considerable knowledge has been accumulated. However, much of the communicated knowledge and recent research results do not go beyond 'the usual suspects' (Finkelstein & Mooney 2003). We should continue to accumulate knowledge and not start from scratch every time we discuss or study boards of directors. We should not only

---

[6] They will hereafter be referred to as the Norefjell workshops.

focus on the easy-to-place pieces in a complicated jigsaw. Studies of the usual suspects are still the most common, but we need to go further. We need to challenge borders. Abraham Maslow's hammer example is famous.[7] He noted that 'if the only tool you have is a hammer, then you tend to see every problem as a nail.' Daily et al. (2003) challenge us to make a joint effort to dismantle the fortresses that are hindering the development of studies of boards of directors. We need to use more tools than the hammer, as the reality is more complex than a nail.

Several review articles have been published during recent decades; many help us understand where we are, and some even help our search for the path forward. The many reviews about boards from management perspectives that have been conducted since the publication of BGV include those about board composition (e.g. Kang, Cheng & Grey 2007), women on boards (e.g. Kirsch 2017; Post & Byron 2015; Terjesen, Singh & Sealy 2009; Wellalage & Locke 2013), corporate social responsibility (CSR) (Byron & Post 2016), boards in family businesses (Bammens, Voordeckers & Gils 2011), boards in emerging economies (Young et al. 2008), company performance (Dalton & Dalton 2011; Finegold, Benson & Hecht 2007), board effectiveness (Petrovic 2008), board tasks (e.g. Aberg et al. 2017; Boivie et al. 2016; Pugliese et al. 2009; Judge & Talaulicar 2017) and board behaviour and behavioural perspectives (Ees, Gabrielsson & Huse 2009; Westphal & Zajac 2013). Reviews are also conducted from disciplines and perspectives outside management, as for example law, finance and accounting (e.g. Oshry, Hermalin & Weisbach 2010).

The recent reviews show increasinging acknowledgement of the importance of understanding context, behaviour and evolution. Examples include Johnson, Schnatterly and Hill's (2013) review on board capital and various reviews about women on boards. The main finding by Post and Byron (Byron & Post 2016; Post & Byron 2015) is the importance of the national context and the

---

[7] www.psychologytoday.com/blog/you-are-not-so-smart/.../maslows-hammer

mediating variables between the number of women on boards and corporate performance.

During the past decade, I have been involved in writing four review articles in addition to an article presenting building blocks for studies about value-creating boards (Huse 2009b):

- Ees et al. (2009) about applying the behavioural theory of the firm to develop a behavioural theory of boards and corporate governance.
- Pugliese et al. (2009) about boards' strategy involvement.
- Åberg et al. (2017) about boards' involvement in service tasks.
- Huse et al. (2011) about changing the research agenda.

The reviews have different objectives and are written in different ways with different co-authors. There exist many reviews about women on boards. I present here conclusions and contributions from some of these reviews.

2.1 Towards a Behavioural Theory of Boards and Corporate Governance

A core contribution in BGV (Huse 2007, chap. 6) is its focus on behavioural approaches. In 2009, Hans van Ees, Jonas Gabrielsson and I published a follow-up on this chapter in a review issue of *Corporate Governance: An International Review*. The objective was to contribute to an alternative to economic approaches to corporate governance, and we took some steps towards developing a behavioural theory of boards and corporate governance. We built on concepts such as 'political bargaining', 'routinization of decision-making', 'satisficing' and 'problemistic search'. In that way, a behavioural theory of boards and governance would focus more on (a) interaction and processes inside and outside the boardroom, (b) decision-making by coalitions of actors and objectives that are the result of political bargaining, and (c) conflicting as well as cooperating interests that are part of the board's decision-making. A consequence of this approach is that research should focus more on actual than on stylized descriptions of board behaviour. The focus should be on problems of coordination and exploration; knowledge creation might become more important than solving conflicts of interest, exploitation and distribution of value. We used a pragmatist approach, and we argued that research using a behavioural perspective also would be more actionable for practitioners.

We indicated the need for a behavioural theory of boards and corporate governance. Jim Westphal and Ed Zajac presented another step towards such a theory in 2013 (Westphal & Zajac 2013). The two of them have made significant contributions for decades in exploring behavioural perspectives about boards of directors. Their review paper is about explicating the mechanisms of socially situated and constituted agency. Their paper and ours have almost the same title, but what then are the differences in these contributions?

One main difference is that we reflected on concepts and consequences with roots in the classical work of Cyert and March and other colleagues (see e.g. Cyert & March 1963; March & Simon 1958). These classic contributions are not even mentioned by Westphal and Zajac. Their objective was to provide an overarching integrating theoretical perspective on corporate governance that incorporates both macro- and micro-causal factors and outcomes. Their contribution is a summary and reflection of their own publications on the topic that have 'demonstrated the relevance of social structural relationships, institutional processes and cognition' (Westphal & Zajac 2013: 607–8). Socially situated and socially constituted are their two core concepts in this framework. Their contributions and suggestions in relation to each of these concepts will clearly be helpful and important for developing the research agenda and understanding factors of corporate governance.

What do the socially situated and socially constituted concepts contain? Socially situated agency is about the context and content of board behaviour. Related to this concept, Westphal and/or Zajac have published studies about social influence through flattering, mentoring and social learning. It is about exchange norms, boundaries and levels and third-party ties and interchange among corporate leaders. Socially situated agency also includes negative reciprocity and avoidance; socially situated constituents, leaders and lower-level managers; the dynamics of the socially situated agency; and social distancing.

Socially constituted or created agency includes micro-social structure and social identification. It is about dyad-level and group-level social creation processes, symbolic management, sociopolitical processes and institutional conformity. It is about determinants of institutional change, negative performance attributes by third parties, the dynamics of micro-social and macro-social formation of groups and processes and, finally, changes in the institutional logics of governance.

2.2   Understanding Board Involvement

The understanding of antecedents and outcomes of board task involvement was an important topic in BGV, and several studies of board involvement or boards' task involvement have appeared during recent years. Pugliese et al. (2009) and Aberg et al. (2017) contribute updates of studies going beyond boards' control or monitoring involvement, and Judge and Talaulicar (2017) present a comprehensive review of board involvement in strategic decision-making processes. The board involvement stream is introduced here. The core characteristic integrating this stream is exploring 'the proper type of involvement by the board to assure the firm's success and longevity' (2017: 51–169). Board involvement and over-involvement are also discussed. Board involvement can be excessive and counterproductive. These authors review the complexity and nature of board involvement.

In the paper by Pugliese et al., we analyzed 150 articles published in 23 management journals. The study contained articles from three time periods: 1972–1989, 1990–2000 and 2001–2007; we showed how research about boards and strategy evolved over time. Topics, theories, settings and sources of data interact and influence insights about how we see strategy relationships during three specific time periods. The review showed how research about boards and strategy evolved from normative and structural approaches to behavioural and cognitive approaches. Our suggestions for a research agenda included examination of institutional and context-specific factors and understanding the importance of boards' strategic involvement when nominating and recruiting board members. We suggested that research be more venturesome in the use of methods so that it can fully capture the impact of board processes and dynamics.

We found a trend towards more pluralism in the board strategy debate. In the third time period, empirical papers were gaining importance; alternative theories started to challenge agency theory; European and Asian samples started to gain importance; and sources of information varied. The development of the journal *Corporate Governance: An International Review* was significant in this period, and some of the changes reflected the policies and practices described in this journal.

In our second task review paper (Aberg et al. 2017), we also discuss strategy when examining the notion of boards and service tasks. Various concepts are used to describe tasks boards typically are involved in, which may contribute to value creation. There are several overlaps between service and strategy. Service as strategy is a concept that has been used to show alternatives to control or monitoring. In this review article, we used an input-process/outcome-context approach.

Judge and Talaulicar (2017) introduced their review by referring to Mace (1971) and Fama and Jensen (1983a), but they used the Pugliese et al. (2009) review as their starting point. The Aberg et al. paper on service tasks uses the Johnson, Daily and Ellstrand (1996) review as starting point. Both reviews are appreciative of the contributions from BGV, the value-creating board framework and the large number of publications that have used the value-creating board instrument (Huse 2009a, 2009c).

2.3 New Perspectives on Board Research: Changing the Research Agenda

Corporate governance is at a crossroad; thus, in Huse et al. (2011) we suggested a revised research agenda. We built our suggestions on three reviews, i.e. Daily et al. (2003), Gabrielsson and Huse (2004) and Hambrick, Werder and Zajac (2008), and we put forth some tenets of a new research stream. Alternative theoretical approaches, alternative research questions and alternative methods were suggested. It was an attempt to show how to do research about actual board behaviour, and how boards may contribute to value creation. When some of the assumptions in agency theory are relaxed, several new pathways for research may arise; in our contribution, we relaxed assumptions about complete contracts and ex ante contracting.

The three reviewed papers presented first that scholars too often have been subject to empirical dogmatism. Second, scholars generally avoid conducting research that is critical of established research models, methods and findings (Daily et al. 2003). Third, particular attention should be paid to context, behaviour and evolution (Gabrielsson & Huse, 2004). Finally, as corporations and social values evolve, so do the boundaries of what constitute governance (Hambrick et al. 2008).

Theories should be employed that broaden the existing scope of research and challenge traditional assumptions about principal-agent relationships. Scholars in strategy, management and organizational behaviour should draw from the rich body of literature existing in these disciplines. Theories we presented for future research were particularly versions of a behavioural theory of the firm (Cyert & March 1963), social identity theory (Ashforth & Meal 1989) and team production theory (Blair & Stout 1999). The different theories have overlapping implications for future research, but we argued that generally in our research we should depart from what we do know and explore what we do not know. This implies the study of context, behaviour and evolution, and the study of board leadership and boards as teams, behavioural structures and processes, as well as powers and influences inside and outside the boardroom.

Methodological issues are addressed as a challenge for the development of our knowledge about boards of directors. Direct links are needed between research questions, theoretical approaches and the methods used. However, we observed that research questions and even theories were chosen based on the empirical data that was available. We also argued in this review for more contextual and contingency studies, the collection of primary data through surveys and the use of processual research and the employment of processual data. Process studies imply changes, and process scholars will need to work across or between levels of analyses to explore the dynamics between relationships at individual, group, organizational and social levels of analyses Huse et al. 2011). Pettigrew describes why and how studies of processes should be conducted as processual studies (Pettigrew 1997; Pye & Pettigrew 2005). Processual studies are like 'catching the reality in flight, to explore the dynamic quality of human conduct and organizational life and to embed such dynamics over time in the various layers of context in which streams of activities occur' (Pettigrew 1997: 342).

2.4   Women on Boards (WoB) Reviews

We also needed to review the literature on women on boards (WoB) and through various papers determine our position and contributions to it. We clearly identified various streams of research on the topic. I often find the following distinctions among research streams useful:

- Benchmarking studies. Comparisons and development of the number of women on boards (e.g. Catalyst 2014; Sealy & Vinnicombe 2012), including intra-firm, inter-firm, national and regional comparisons. Comparisons are often made over time.
- Getting women on boards studies. One subgroup of studies looks at the importance of institutional backgrounds and traditions in

determining the number of women on boards (e.g. Grosvold & Brammer 2011), including studies about obstacles in business and society, and studies using various feminist perspectives. Studies about leakages in the talent pipeline may be found here. Another subgroup studies the effects of public policy initiatives (e.g. Iannotta et al. 2016; Teigen 2012; Vos & Culliford 2014), including also the effects of quotas. Many of the studies about the Norwegian quota legislation for increasing the number of women on boards are also within this stream. Dynamic studies about the processes of getting women on boards are a third subgroup (e.g. Seierstad, et al. 2017).

- Business case studies for women on boards, including both input-output as well as input-process–output-context approaches (e.g. Byron & Post 2016; Post & Byron 2015). Most of these studies are quantitative, but qualitative studies are also found.
- Studies about the board members, who they are and how women may be different from men (e.g. Huse 2011a; Rigolini et al. 2017), including also studies of motivation and preferences. Many of the studies of gender related dynamics may be placed here.

Despite the large research interest on the topic of women on boards, I have not found studies linking the various perspectives.

2.5 Summary and Conclusion

The reviews presented earlier generally conclude that most research about boards of directors is still using input-output approaches with variables or concepts similar to the 'usual suspects'. Agency theory is still the dominant theoretical perspective. However, we can observe some trends:

- Agency theory studies are being questioned and studies are using alternative sets of theories.
- More studies are using input-process–output-context approaches.
- Holistic and processual studies and the understanding of actors are being recognized.

- Studies identify the importance of identities and behaviour of individual actors and groups of actors.
- Studies conducted by researchers from outside the United States are increasing. The hegemony of US data is being reduced, and many European-based studies rely on survey data.

The development of research about boards of directors may be observed through distinguishing among various research streams. These streams are partly following the trends pointed out earlier, but they are also displayed through the variations in dissemination outlets and research networks. Certain outlets attract certain types of research and research efforts. For example, correlations seem to exist between specific journals and studies by various networks of researchers.[8] During the past decade, *Corporate Governance: An International Review* has become an important outlet for research about boards and corporate governance. This journal is particularly important for research that does not directly fit into the major US-based journals. *Journal of Business Ethics* has become an important outlet for studies about women on boards.

3   Factors of Value-Creating Boards: Challenging Borders

In terms of the challenges facing boards and governance, Chris Pierce (2016) offers one recent projection regarding trends in corporate governance:

- *Increased use of corporate governance (CG) codes*
- *Higher level of regulation and enforcement*
- *Greater board diversity*
- *More focus on strategy, value creation and corporate responsibility*
- *Greater emphasis on the governance of risk*

---

[8] The main US-based journals for publications on empirical board research are *Academy of Management Journal, Strategic Management Journal, Administrative Science Quarterly, Journal of Management* and *Organization Science*. Each of these journals may be observed to be related to certain research streams and researcher networks.

- *Greater emphasis on information governance*
- *Greater emphasis on compensation governance*
- *Greater emphasis on accountability and responsibility to shareholders and other stakeholders*
- *Increased use of board evaluations and board performance development*
- *Director and board development*

I appreciate many of the insights and experiences presented here by Pierce, but my input is still different and I do not completely agree with his presentation. I will here present six sets of factors about boards, governance and value creation. On one side, my factors are narrower as my focus is on value-creating boards and not on corporate governance. On the other side, my factors are responses to challenging borders in research and practice. The factors follow from the previous sections, and they reflect the topics I recommend my PhD students and other junior faculty to have high on their research agendas. These factors are also high on my agenda when challenging and communicating with business people and board members about developing value-creating boards.

The understanding of corporate governance and boards of directors is at a crossroad, and it is a challenge to find the best route to our destination. Main crossroads are where research meets business, where past meets future and where micro meets macro. It is not easy to make the best choices, but it is important to understand that it matters which choice we are making. We need to understand the importance of values, the future, theory, individuals, business and society. I have thus decided to group the various factors of boards, governance and value creation in the following way:

1. Theorizing about value-creating boards.
2. Involvement of boards where they add the most value.
3. Preparing for the future and the digital transformation of society.
4. Going beyond the surface: understanding actors and dynamics.

5. Diversity and women on boards: the business case.
6. When micro meets macro: contributing in actual discourses.

The chosen factors are challenging corporate governance borders by continually focusing on values, people, language, cognition, perspectives and dynamics, and they contribute to designing a future-oriented, holistic and value-based agenda for research and practice. The factors should challenge us to contribute to shape the future.

3.1   Factor 1

Theorizing about Value-Creating Boards

Yet, the goal of turning the board into an effective, productive team is not only possible – it's essential. (Nadler 2004)

> *Challenges*
> What is corporate governance and what is the role of the board? This factor contributes to a theory that might integrate inputs about the role of the board with lessons and theories from strategy and leadership. Boards and corporate governance have benefitted during recent years from inputs from agency theory. However, the influence of agency theory is disputed. A board that serves has for some time been presented as an alternative to a board that monitors and controls. However, I argue here for a model of boards that lead and of team leadership. Observations about actual board behaviour clearly show the impact of strategy and leadership research, but this richness is not appreciated in mainstream board research.

> **Key words:** contribution to value creation, an alternative to agency theory, teams and leadership

3.1.1   A Grand Theory of Corporate Governance?

There have been renewed calls for a grand theory of corporate governance. Agency theory has been used during recent decades as the bible of corporate governance. Core assumptions in this bible are that humans are sinners (opportunism in the corporate governance terminology) and that Adam and Eve were exposed to limited and asymmetric information, as they had to leave Paradise. Agency theory has been severely criticized by many scholars for its too simplistic assumptions and for its negative consequences on business and society (e.g. Ghoshal 2005). Furthermore, boards of directors existed centuries or even millenniums before the letters[9] introducing agency theory were presented. There have therefore also been calls for or a search for alternative grand theories of corporate governance.

Stewardship theory (Donaldson 1990) abolished the opportunism assumption, and it was introduced as an alternative to agency theory. A board that serves became a main concept and contribution in stewardship theory. However, the theory was weakened in 1997 (Davis, Schoorman & Donaldson 1997), as the core stewardship theory advocates introduced a mild form of opportunism.

Stakeholder perspectives have also been presented as an alternative theory. In 1998, Bengt Johannisson helped me reflect on the use of a theory of paternalism to explore governance in family firms (see e.g. Johannisson & Huse 2000), and in 2002, Anna Grandori[10] challenged me to do more work on team production theory. However, will we ever have a grand theory of corporate governance?

One of the theoretical contributions I find the most promising is the development of the extended version of the team production theory. Various colleagues and I have put most of our energy for theory development in this area. We started with developing

---

[9] There are four articles (letters) that generally have been considered to be those introducing agency theory. These are Jensen and Meckling (1976), Fama (1980), Fama and Jensen (1983a) and (1983b) plus a fifth article that there is less agreement on. I have considered Jensen and Ruback (1983) as a pillar in developing agency theory.

[10] In 2002, Anna Grandori invited me together with Margaret Blair and William Aoki to an event in Milan. See Grandori (2004). The inputs for the three of them started my initiatives to develop the extended team production approach. The development of this approach has been done in collaboration with several colleagues - particularly Jonas Gabrielsson, but also Anna Grandori, Robert Hoskisson, Alessandro Minichilli and Silke Machold.

a team production approach after receiving various inputs from Margareth Blair, William Aoki and Anna Grandori, and we hoped to find an approach that could help us theoretically link law and economics on the one side with approaches from leadership and strategy on the other. We labelled the approach 'extended' because we found team production as presented by Blair and Stout (1999, 2001) and later also by Kaufmann and Englander (2005) to be fairly static. These authors did not properly address human behaviour and behavioural perspectives. Here is a summary of core factors in the extended team production development:

- Using property right theory and not agency theory constitutes the background from law and economics. In property rights theory, in contrast to agency theory, it is argued that instead of making multilateral contracts among all actors in joint production, a central common party (a team) should make bilateral contracts with the various input providers.
- A team production theory builds on the assumption that firms are separate and independent moral entities, and that the main task of the board is to create long-term values and sustainable competitive advantage in the firm.
- The extended version of the team production theory is dynamic and includes implications in relation to strategic management and organizational behaviour. The extended version of team production theory integrates cooperative game theory and the behavioural theory of the firm.

3.1.2   Team Production Theory as Described in Law and Economics

Team production theory has its background in property rights theory (Alchian & Demsetz 1972) and has been extended, developed and adapted to understand corporate governance (Blair & Stout 1999; Kaufmann & Englander 2005). Property rights theory is a team production theory, and proponents of property rights theory have argued that instead of only representing the interest of the shareholders, boards should also represent those stakeholders who add value, assume unique risk and possess strategic information (Blair 1995; Blair & Stout 1999; Grandori 2004; Kaufmann & Englander 2005). Those contributing the most to value creation should be in control.

Team production theory is embedded in the view of organization as a nexus of team-specific assets where stakeholders are seen as investing firm-specific resources with the hope of profiting from team production (Gabrielsson & Huse 2009). The team production approach conceptualizes the board as a mediating hierarchy assigned the overall purpose of leading the firm forwards by providing a balanced and long-term perspective of value creation activities.

Team production focuses on the upside of value creation, decisions are the result of processes and board members are impartial and involved. A main task for board members is to support firm-specific investments. A team production approach has a strong focus on stakeholders commitment.

The board of directors is in this theory identified as playing a critical role as an impartial mediator between a firm's value-adding stakeholders. If a board cannot uphold this ideal, for example by consistently favouring a particular group of stakeholder over others, the theory posits that there will be concerns from value-adding stakeholders that the returns from firm-specific investments will not be fairly distributed. This will reduce their interest in investing in firm-specific resources; over time, this will limit the firm's ability to compete effectively in the marketplace. As such, the board of directors is seen as a critical coordinating body whose main task is to represent and mediate between all stakeholders that add value, assume unique risk and possess strategic information relevant for firm operations. At the same time, it needs to channel the expertise and knowledge by which the firm competes into the strategic decision-making process.

We argue that a team production model of corporate governance makes a better fit than agency theory with contemporary thinking. It emphasizes resources and capabilities as main sources of sustained competitive advantage. We also argue that an extended version of team production theory does not only analyze the attributes and structural characteristics of boards but will also direct attention to and emphasize the role of well-functioning working structures and processes in and around the boardroom for boards' ability to create value.

3.1.3   Contributions to an Extended Version of Team Production Theory

Our work to develop and conceptualize the extended team production theory contains several publications, including the following:

- Gabrielsson, Huse and Minichilli (2007): Understanding the leadership role of the board chairperson through a team production approach.
- Gabrielsson and Huse (2009): Boards of directors and corporate innovation.
- Huse, Gabrielsson and Minichilli (2009b): Improving corporate governance practices.
- Huse, Hoskisson, Zattoni and Vigano (2011): New perspectives on board research – changing the research agenda.
- Machold, Huse, Minichilli and Nordqvist (2011): Board leadership and strategy involvement in small firms – a team production approach.
- Huse and Gabrielsson (2012): Board leadership and value creation – an extended team production approach.
- Gabrielsson, Calabro and Huse (2016): Boards and value creation in family firms – an extended team production approach.

Each of these papers makes a distinct contribution to the development of an extended approach of team production theory. In Gabrielsson et al. (2007), we argue that effective board performance is driven by the extent to which corporate directors bring relevant knowledge to the board. An important prerequisite, however, is that the knowledge must be used. We contend that the competencies and behaviours of the board chairperson are critical to unleash a board's value-creating potential. The paper provides empirical support for a team production approach in relation to board leadership.

Theories should be employed that broaden the existing scope of research and challenge traditional assumptions about the principal-agent relationship. This was our starting point in Huse et al. (2011), and we argue that team production theory meets some of the shortcomings in agency theory. Gabrielsson and Huse (2009) provide an extensive presentation of what we labelled a 'modern team production theory', and it offers empirical support to the theory. A process-oriented culture is associated with boards' participation in the whole strategy process, while a decision-oriented culture is associated with arms-length strategy ratification and control. We empirically studied the application of team production theory to entrepreneurial firms. In Huse et al. (2009), we attempt to show how a team production approach to boards can help develop peak performing organizations.

In Huse and Gabrielsson (2012), we argue that there is a lack of focus on board leadership in the academic corporate governance debate, and we introduce and apply the extended version of the team production theory. The core in Machold et al. (2011) is the importance of leadership, and we attempted to integrate the leadership literature into the literature about boards and corporate governance. For this objective, we use the extended team production approach. In this approach, board leadership is positively related to the board's strategy involvement in small firms.

The objective of Gabrielsson et al. (2016) is to take a step in developing and disseminating the extended version of team production theory as a way to better understand how boards may contribute to value creation in family firms. The development of a boardroom culture that favours team production may be a challenge in a family business as family or friendship ties often link board members.

3.1.4 Extended Team Production Theory

Compared to team production theory from law and economics, in the extended version we attempt theoretically and empirically to apply the theory to strategic management and organizational behaviour. Table 1 shows the core characteristics of the extended version of team production theory compared to similar characteristics in agency theory. The table is based on Gabrielsson and Huse (2009: 231).

The extended team production theory for understanding boards and governance leans heavily on cooperating game theory (Aoki 1984) in its long-term perspective of value creation. Such a perspective rejects short-sighted distribution rules for the benefit of one particular group of stakeholders. A core issue for promoting and sustaining firm-specific investments via the governance system is coping with problems of free riding and shirking. The extended team production approach rejects both ex ante division rules and ex post bargaining as effective solutions to deal with the problem of free riding and shirking (Gabrielsson et al. 2016).

The main role of boards in team production theory is to contribute to sustainable value creation. This implies a focus on the upside of value creation without forgetting the governance side. The selection of board members will be based on their competence, impartiality and willingness to be involved.

The team production model of corporate governance suggests that boards should be composed of a diverse set of board members who can knowledgeably express their interests, perspectives and expertise to value-adding stakeholders. Board members must consequently work together as a team and share their knowledge and skills in a productive setting to enhance their collective efforts and decision-making abilities. Moreover, as no board member is likely to possess the full complement of information and knowledge necessary to achieve the multiple strategic goals of the firm, working together as a team may permit greater productivity than that achieved by individual board members' efforts.

In a board setting, a team production approach will postulate that the productivity of any board member is greater because of the interaction with other board members. Board members are

Table 1 Agency theory vs. the extended team production theory

	Agency Theory	Extended Team Production Theory
What is a firm?	Nexus of contracts	Nexus of team-specific assets
Main purpose of a firm?	Maximize return to shareholders	Value creation through team production
Main role of boards?	Reducing costs of managerial opportunism and distribute values back to shareholders	Contribute to sustainable value creation
Value creation activities	Focus on down side: limiting the destruction of value	Focus on up side: supporting the creation of value (e.g. through innovation)
Primary board member qualifications?	Independent and detached	Competence, impartial and involved
Strategy process	Arms-length involvement in ratification and monitoring of strategic decisions	Close involvement in the whole process: formulating, ratifying, executing and evaluating
Board culture	Decision oriented: characterized by criticality and a questioning attitude	Process oriented: Characterized by open and generous discussions related to diverse knowledge inputs and opposing viewpoints

complementing each other rather than serving as substitutes for each other (Gabrielsson & Huse 2007). The team production approach highlights the need for skilled and competent board chairperson leadership.

3.1.5 Summary and Conclusions

I find that working with property rights theory and team production is a promising path, and this may give legitimacy for doing impactful research about boards of directors. The extended version contributes to integrating lessons from strategy and leadership, and it increases its application to practice.

Creating value for the firm does not need to be in conflict with creating value for the management, shareholders or other stakeholders. Using this perspective, all stakeholders will in the end be better off than when using agency theory-based approaches. Applying and using team production theory may contribute to creating shared values and reducing pay gap concerns.[11]

3.2 Factor 2

Involvement of Boards Where They Add the Most Value

'*Is your company's board of directors creating value – or destroying it? (Directors and Boards)*[12]

Challenges
Boards should place their efforts so that they create the most values. Following a research tradition where the firm is the objective, a distinction is made between value creation and value distribution.

---

[11] See e.g. Porter and Kramer (2011) or the documentary Inequality for all (2013) by Robert Reich (http://www.imdb.com/title/tt2215151/).

[12] This was the heading in the *Directors and Boards Magazine* 23.4.2014. The magazine presented an executive training program at Wharton Executive Education. This training program was developed around the book *Boards that Lead* (Charan et al. 2014), and the program was about corporate governance that creates value.

However, creating sustainable values may also imply sharing value creation with all stakeholders.

Board performance should be measured based on its contribution to value creation and not by its involvement in different tasks. Value creation, tasks and the use of resources need to be aligned. This may be achieved by applying core factors from the strategy literature, including value chain and resource approaches. Value-creating tasks and capabilities are identified.

Keywords: shared value, sustainable value creation, value chain, strategy literature

3.2.1 Creating Shared Values

My perspective on value creation has two aspects. The first is from strategic management: the board should contribute to create long-term sustainable rent or competitive advantage for the company. The second is that the board contributes to a positive and sustainable society.

Michael Porter (Porter & Kramer 2011) argues that companies today are trapped in an outdated approach to value creation. During past decades, value creation has been viewed narrowly with a focus on optimizing short-term financial performance. The broader influences that determine the longer-term success of the company are forgotten. For example, the successful young Norwegian oil company Aker BP has clearly indicated that its success is dependent on having the best suppliers, but Aker BP is instrumental in making them the best.[13] Companies need to have a long-term perspective in relation to all stakeholders: companies and stakeholders can make each other better.

The principle of shared value goes even further. It involves creating economic values in such a way that it also creates values for society. Porter argues that one of the ways that companies can create shared values is by redefining productivity in the value chain.

---

[13] The story is based on a presentation in winter 2017 by the CEO of Aker BP Karl Johnny Hersvik.

3.2.2   A Value-Chain Approach to Value Creation

How can the board be a strategic advantage to your company? My overall argument, as indicated earlier, is that boards should contribute to long-term sustainable societal value creation. However, even though this may be easy to communicate, it may be difficult to measure and enact. I have therefore learnt to use my perspective as a strategy scholar and summarize the BGV book from a value-chain approach (Huse 2007: 283–92). A value-chain approach has proved to be valuable for communicating ways values are created. The core of the value-chain approach is that values are identified and measured in intermediate steps. Values may in general be measured from input activities, via production, through decision-making and control to output activities. The argument is, then, that boards should be involved where they add the most value.

In this approach, board members need to reflect on the values the company creates, and which tasks board members may be involved in to contribute to the sustainability of those values. The board value-chain perspective and the value-chain framework have been refined in several publications (Gabrielsson et al. 2016; Huse 2013; Huse & Gabrielsson 2012; Huse et al. 2009a, 2009b; Huse & Søland 2009), and the framework has been applied in various contexts. It has become one of my main tools in communicating the value-creating board concepts to students and practitioners. A general version of the framework is presented in the Figure 1.

This is a sorting framework of concepts from BGV. It appeared for the first time in 2005; since then it has been frequently used as a tool for board evaluations. Several consultancies have used it for developing their evaluation tools. It has further been developed through theoretical reflections and empirical data. Theoretically, it has been used as a tool for sorting theories about boards and board tasks. Empirically, it has been tested on Norwegian data from the value-creating board instrument (Huse & Søland 2009). The instrument has an impact on sorting concepts and relationships about boards of directors. This is the framework most of my executive training sessions are building on. It relates board activities to value creation.

VALUE CREATION	Inbound logistics	Operation	Innovation and development	Resource allocation	Risk management and implementation	Outbound logistics
TASKS	Legitimacy, network, lobbying	Advisory and support	Strategic management and collaboration	Strategic control and decision-making	Internal control and compensation	Output control, CSR-control and embedding
RESOURCES	Social and relational capital	Functional and general competence	Diversity	Decisions-making and analytical	Business and board experience	Integrity, negotiating and mediating
GROUP EFFECTIVENESS	Preparations and involvement	Openness and generosity	Creativity, preparations, cognitive conflicts, cohesiveness	Decision-orientation	Critical attitudes, preparations, cognitive conflicts	Inde-pendence
LEADER	Figurehead	Mentor and supporter	Leader and motivator	Strategist	Chair	Liaison and moderator
STRUCTURES	Recruitment evaluations	Introductions and training	"Away.days" Development evaluations	Rules and structures	Work descriptions Committees Alone meetings	Ethics- and stakeholder documents Report evaluations

Figure 1 A value-chain approach to value-creating-boards

3.2.3   Industrial Organization and the Resource Literature

The framework is embedded in the strategy literature and goes beyond the value chain and the industrial organization approach. We also attempt to use resource approaches to achieve competitive advantage and sustainable rents through the development of boards of directors.

The board members are typically considered the resources or capital boards have. Considerable energy has thus been spent to identify characteristics of board members. The two characteristics that have traditionally been given the most attention are independence and competence. The composition of the board as a whole has also been addressed. The most attention has been given to tangible resources – something that is easy to identify and imitate. However, sustainable advantage or rent is achieved through unique intangible resources. Such resources, or in this case competences, are described in the value chain in Figure 1. The resource approach has additional steps, namely related to knowledge (Grant 1996), core competency (Hamel & Prahalad 1990), dynamic capabilities (Teece, Pisano & Shuen 1997) and absorptive capacity (Zahra & George 2002). The value-chain logic also implies that these resources should be linked to variations in the tasks related to the value chain. Furthermore, the resources should not only exist but also be used. Here we have the link to leadership and team theories, including the extended team production approach.

I find the concepts related to absorptive capacity and dynamic capability of particular interest for creating sustainable values through the board. Thus, we have recently been putting these concepts high up on our research agenda about value-creating boards, and we have used the Norwegian value-creating board database in studies focusing on these concepts.[14] The sensing, seizing and configuring of capabilities are important concepts from the dynamic capabilities perspective. Exploratory, transformative and exploitative

---

[14] The work on absorptive capacity was used in the PhD theses' of Aud Schønning (2014) and Pingying Zhang Wenstøp (2008), while dynamic managerial capabilities were important in the PhD thesis of Carl Åberg (2017).

learning concepts are important from an absorptive capacity perspective. These issues are all important for the board's involvement in strategy development and decision-making.

3.2.4 Decision-making Group

It may be argued that boards are not teams. Board typically meet infrequently, the chair cannot instruct the other board members regarding their involvement and decision-making, the board is collegially responsible and the board members are often all highly respected and experienced persons (see e.g. Forbes & Milliken 1999). This description indicates that it is difficult to have boards work as teams. However, the value-chain framework presented earlier indicates that it is important from a value-creating perspective that boards act like teams. David Nadler (2004) wrote that the higher you get into an organization, the more difficult teaming becomes, but turning the board into a team is not only possible but also essential.

A 'team' may be defined as a group of people working together for a joint objective. Team characteristics of cohesiveness, creativity and cognitive conflict are all important. The same is true of openness and generosity, preparation and involvement, criticality and independence. The challenges to developing boards into teams are thus big, and the main responsibility falls on board leadership and structure.

Not all board activities or board tasks require team efforts, and several tasks do not even need to be conducted inside the boardroom. There are tasks that by their nature will take place outside the boardroom, while there are other tasks that should take place outside. These differences show that a board chair may take on different roles depending on the board tasks that are being conducted. Board leadership and board structures may support efforts to turn the competencies of the board members into core competencies and capabilities.

3.2.5 Ambidexterity

'Ambidexterity' is a concept used to show that multiple activities may be conducted at the same time. It is based on the idea that each hand may be used simultaneously for different tasks. It is often related to the ability to achieve high levels of exploration and exploitation.

I wrote my PhD thesis about twenty-five years ago.[15] The thesis was about solving the paradoxes in board-management relationships and exploring the various approaches that may be used to solve the apparent paradoxes. The approaches include separations in time and space, including contextual, reciprocal and cyclical solutions. I tried to solve the simultaneous need for distance and closeness by defining them not on one dimension but by describing distance or closeness on two dimensions. I thus argued for the need to combine independence and interdependence, distrust and trust, male and female, yin and yang as well as control and service. Today I would have presented the solving of the paradoxes within an ambidexterity framework with a structural approach. A decision-oriented culture may thus also be combined with a process-oriented culture (Huse 2007: 234), and short-term perspectives may be combined with long-term perspectives.

3.2.6 Summary and Conclusions

Boards should not be defined by the tasks they are performing, but how they create value. The value-chain model integrates strategy perspectives from industrial organization and resource approaches. The value-chain model has contributed to the sorting of concepts. A next step will be to develop propositions and theories. The development of extended version of the team production theory is one such step.

---

[15] The thesis was based on an empirical study and written as a monograph in the Norwegian language. The thesis was published in 1994 and its title was 'Distansert nærhet: En studie om betydningen av relasjonene mellom styre og ledelse for faktisk styrearbeid'. However, several articles related to it were published in English. Many of them are cited in BGV, e.g. Huse (1993) ('Relational Norms as Supplement to Neo-classical Understandings of Directorates') and Huse (1994b) ('Board-management Relations in Small Firms: The Paradox of Simultaneous Independence and Interdependence).

3.3   Factor 3

Preparing for the Future and the Digital Transformation of Society

Find an experienced digitizer and add that person to the board of directors. A digital hand on the board can help dramatically in an organization's transformation. He or she can advise the CEO, help to guide major investments, monitor progress toward digital goals, and make connections to other organizations with similar issues. A board member won't oversee day-to-day digital projects, but can provide resources and motivation to help them succeed. (*Thomas Davenport,* Wall Street Journal)[16]

Challenges
We are daily meeting challenges related to digitalization. We see the development of social media and the importance of cyber security. However, what are the critical factors students, business leaders and board members need to relate to? In BGV I did not present challenges related to the digital transformation of the society. Today this is one of the core factors of boards, governance and value creation.

Key words: future of boards and corporations, digital era, sustainability, virtual organizations, shared economy

3.3.1   Preparing for the Future: Megatrends and Paradigm Shifts

A main factor for developing value-creating boards is the inclusion of perspectives relating to the future. What will boards look like in the future? And how will they be able to contribute to value creation in business and society? We cannot expect that businesses and society will be the same in twenty years as they are today. Major transformations of businesses and society are taking place, and consequences for corporations and corporate governance in the next five years may be tremendous. Corporate governance recommendations, businesses, board members and research cannot only

---

[16] Thomas Davenport in *Wall Street Journal*, 22 February 2016: 'Why Boards of Directors Need a Digital Leader'. https://blogs.wsj.com/experts/2016/02/22/why-boards-of-directors-need-a-digital-leader/ downloaded 26 March 2018

pay attention to what may happen in the future but also actively prepare for it. We are at all levels facing challenges with respect to the increased importance of cyber security, social media and the shared economy.

An overarching question about the future is the consequence of digitalization. This issue is not about board procedures and tools that may support boards. It is not either only about the need for boards or corporation to include digital awareness and knowledge in their decision-making. It is about the transformation of society, including the transformation of corporations. Boundaryless and virtual organizations have been on the agenda in research and teaching for some decades, but consequences for boards and corporate governance have only received limited attention. I argue that we will face a major paradigm shift about boards and governance as a result of these quickly escalating digital developments.

The digital developments have consequences on many fronts and interface with other megatrends. These include the replacement of financial capital as a bottleneck factor with human and social capital for business development. New and alternative ways of communication and influencing are appearing, including the role of social media. The digital developments have consequences for geography, globalization and internationalization. It has consequences for gender and inclusion in the workforce and career advancement as well as gender equality in society. Even the human body may be directly influenced by digital developments. If we believe in certain values, then we cannot just sit and wait for the consequences to come. We need to explore now the challenges and possibilities, and the earlier we act, the larger the possibilities we will have an influence on the direction and consequences of this avalanche that obviously is on the way.

We say that it is difficult to predict – particularly about the future, but I may use an example about my stepson Didrik. Without money, but with lots of ideas, guts and initiatives, he and some fellow engineering students established FlowMotion

Technologies.[17] They developed a gimbal to capture smooth cinematic videos with smartphones. They started prototyping in April 2015 and teamed up with a manufacturing partner with experience in consumer electronics, including assembling, packaging and on-the-ground support in China. During fall 2016, they started a kick-starter campaign; by its close in the beginning of January 2017, more than 5,500 backers pledged a total of more than 1.3 million USD to help FlowMotion ONE go live. Offices were established in California and in Norway. Their most important assets were ideas, guts, energy and communication creativity and skills. How should they develop their company, boards and governance structures? I will argue that they may benefit from a board that includes sponsors, mentors and advisors who can guide them through growth and development challenges. They may benefit from help in reflecting on and checking risks and regulations. Crowdfunding and crowdsourcing have made it possible for these students to create a global success story. The challenge is to create a governance structure around the energy and brains of a few students.

3.3.2 Four Levels of Boards and Digitalization

Boards will change in various ways and for various reasons due to digitalization (Bankewitz, Aberg & Teuchert 2016). A first level of change concerns board processes and procedures. Enabling technologies that arise will change behaviours. Boards will be equipped with both software and hardware that may facilitate and ease their work but also change known and studied board behaviour. A second level of changes is about digital knowledge and mindsets. Digital quotas on boards have been suggested. This means that board members should be recruited based on their digital competence. It is not only about digital knowledge but also about how to create cultures of understanding digitalization. Boards needs a digital mindset to communicate in a meaningful way with senior management: the board can help the company understand the

---

[17] See for example www.facebook.com/FlowMotionTech.

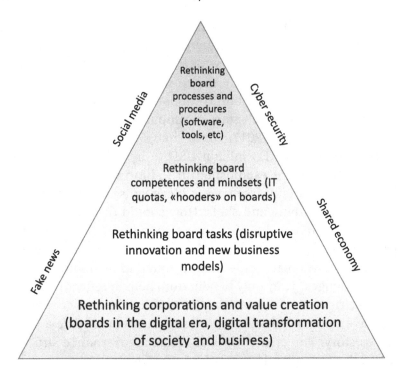

Figure 2 Boards and four levels of digitalization

impact technology changes are having and will have on the business. A third level is about business models. We in business and society are experiencing disruption and radical innovation and challenges, and much of our previous experiences and understandings are quickly becoming outdated. Even in the short run, boards are challenged to leverage disruptive innovation change processes and structures – and even the whole approach of doing business. A fourth level of changes concerns changes in corporate and organizational forms and regulations. This also includes the role of investors and the time horizon of investors. The different levels are presented in Figure 2. The four levels in Figure 2 are surrounded by various challenges, for example, the challenges from the shared economy, social media, cybersecurity and fake news.

Will boards of directors be needed in the future? Who will be board members and what will they do? How should corporate governance guidelines be changed to provide and safeguard sustainable value creation for business and society? Are we even sure that in few years we are going to have corporations as we see them today? Will we enter an era of virtual organizations where the value creation may take place in student dormitories or even in bedrooms?

3.3.3 Formal Requirements about Boards

It has been argued for some time that boards are no longer an important tool in corporate governance (Thomsen 2008). Investors and major stakeholders are getting their information and using their influence without using the board. In Norway, a committee suggesting reforms of the Norwegian private limited company law is questioning the needs for formal boards and formal reporting. Formal reporting may not be important as most important stakeholders use digital means and have much more information about the firm than any formal reporting can provide. We already see how our businesses and private lives are followed through various direct marketing efforts based on knowledge about our habits.

Facing some of these challenges, we should try to understand the consequences for boards and corporate governance of this digital transformation of business and society. These consequences should be understood today, as this transformation is like a snowball that already has started rolling down from the mountain, and we know that at some point an avalanche or a revolution in corporate governance will take place. Today we still may have some possibilities to influence the direction of this snowball. On one side, we need to explore how businesses, boards and corporate governance will be influenced by the digital transformation. Its consequences may not be many years in the future. Complete transformation may take place even within few decades. On the other side, we should explore ways we can influence the direction and development of this avalanche so that it does not harm the core values we want to see in the society.

3.3.4   Paradigm Shift

It is urgent that the escalating digital transformation is recognized as having consequences for the development of corporate governance codes and practices, as well as for research and teaching relating to ownership, governance and leadership. Businesses and business schools cannot pretend that these changes will not take place. The digitalization momentum has been unleashed, and we will not be able to stop it. Our challenge is to do our research and teaching with open eyes, and not to close them because we do not know how to deal with this universe.

Digitalization is not only about possibilities and advantages. There may be many disruptive effects, maladaptions (Barnet & O'Neill 2010) and unintended consequences (Ogburn 1922). The digital transformation of society may change the fundamentals of how to create and deliver value. The ongoing digital revolutions will require rethinking of innovation, dynamic capabilities and trust. There is need not only for digital competency on boards and in corporation but also in humans and society.

3.3.5   Summary and Conclusions

Will we during the coming years see a new form of capitalism (see e.g. Davis 2013) or will capitalism be replaced by something else? Porter argues for reinventing capitalism to unleash a wave of innovation and growth. His recipe is to create shared value and the CSV (corporate shared values) concept. We face arguments that 'capitalism is under siege' (Porter & Kramer 2011). The legitimacy of business has fallen to levels not seen recently.

Together with most people in Europe I was extremely concerned to see that it was possible for Donald Trump to become president of the United States. However, we are seeing similar trends of populism in Europe. My concern is that the roots and consequences of this populism will create a destructive economic and societal imbalance in society. This is a major corporate governance challenge, and we need to find and fight the causes leading to this development. We need to find alternatives.

Robert Reich delivered some famous thought-provoking lectures about inequality for all.[18] He spoke about the increasing pay gap in corporations in the United States between those earning the most and the majority of employees. It is about 'money, money, money' and 'the winner takes it all'. His observation is that the middle class is disappearing. The remuneration to corporate top leaders and shareholders is skyrocketing, while there are considerable lay-offs and salary cuts among lower-level and middle-level employees. He argued that corporate leaders who used to be corporate statespersons were replaced with corporate butchers. All gains for growth are now distributed to the top, while the middle class is being cut away from American society. Reich argues about a society in imbalance and that this increasing pay gap is a major threat to the welfare and equality for us all.

I argue that this increasing pay gap is supported by the present dominant corporate governance logic. This logic emphasizes shareholder supremacy and is built on short-termism. One of the consequences of this logic is that cost reductions are given more attention than value creation. The short-term benefits of cost reductions under the present corporate governance paradigm are not used to support value-creating initiatives, but to increase the pay gap. It should be one of our charges in business schools and for responsible citizens to replace this logic by something that is sustainable.

We as corporate governance scholars should together with e.g. OECD and the G20 group put more emphasis on understanding the consequences of digitalization and the development of the financial markets. It is urgent to find ways that may help us avoid the robbing and raping by barbarians.[19] These barbarians may not even be able to understand the language and importance of

---

[18] Reich is Professor at University of California at Berkley and previous secretary of labor under President Bill Clinton. See his blog robertreich.org and his film *Inequality for All*. See also Davis and Cobb (2010).

[19] In my Norwegian textbook (Huse 2011b) as well as in BGV, I present the Vikings in corporate governance.

sustainable value creation for business and society. They may force business cultures into fraud or shortcuts to meet unachievable key performance indicators.

3.4   Factor 4

Going beyond the Surface: Understanding Actors and Dynamics

From the bedroom to the boardroom: The power of erotic capital. (Cathrine Hakim 2011)

Challenges
Among the core contributions from BGV were the emphasis on micro-level approaches and on understanding the human side of boards and governance. In my presentation of this fourth factor, I will argue that we can learn much from sociology, social psychology and psychology for understanding these actors. My recent research efforts have tried to identify and understand core actors, their motivations and their interactions. I used a micro-level approach (mentoring advocates) to understand how individual actors could contribute to influence boards, gender equality and public policies.

The chapter in the centre of BGV was about interactions. Using behavioural perspectives of boards and governance, it introduced the importance of trust, power and influence. The dynamics of micro strategizing and politicking were also highlighted. Here I will provide increased depth to the understanding actors and the dynamics of their interactions. I will not only focus on who the persons on boards are, but I will also argue that it is important to know the types of persons who are not on boards. Concepts from Bourdieu such as 'habitus' and 'capitals' are introduced.

Keywords: social capital, habitus, identification, preference theory

3.4.1   The Human Side of Corporate Governance
The subtitle of BGV is 'The Human Side of Corporate Governance', and behavioural perspectives are a core contribution to this factor. However, many additional approaches and theories have been

introduced since the publication of BGV. Some of our recent contributions follow:

- The understanding of life trajectories (Seierstad et al. 2016).
- Identity, social identity and identification (see e.g. Melkumov, Breit & Khoreva 2015).
- Psychological approaches (e.g. Möltner et al. 2017).
- Power and experience (see e.g. Goldeng 2017).
- Lean in and gender codes (see e.g. Huse et al. 2017).

At one time, I was co-presenting speeches with a gynaecologist. She spoke about women on boards. Her presentation was about chromosomes, genes and hormones. She talked about x- and y-chromosomes, and in her presentation she told about what individuals would be like if they had additional x- or y-chromosomes. Sometimes it would be difficult to distinguish a man from a woman. The conclusion was that if we want to experience and understand actors, diversity and behavioural perspectives, then we need to go beyond the surface. It is not always easy to distinguish women's characteristics from those of men. The differences among men and among women may be larger than those between the sexes.

3.4.2   The Telenor Case

The Telenor Group is a world-leading international Norwegian-based telecommunications corporation. During fall 2016, a conflict between the board chair (Ms Gunn Wærsted) and the CEO and president (Mr Sigve Brekke) became publicly visible, and the chair told Mr Brekke to resign. The CEO rejected this request and approached the board for a decision. The board gave formal support to the CEO.

The CEO had a long background at Telenor, and he had been president of some the fastest-growing subsidiaries in Asia, and during the spring 2015 he was appointed CEO of the whole Telenor group. His appointment was disputed. Telenor is a publicly listed corporation, but the Norwegian State through the Ministry of Industry and Fishery is the majority shareholder.

Norway had a conservative right-wing government, and the conservative Ms Monica Mæland was minister of industry and fishery. The Norwegian government had been strongly criticized for not appointing women as CEOs and board chairs in corporations that were owned or controlled by the state. Strong voices in media required actions by the minister, and many arguments against the new CEO came to the surface. This criticism was also important as the previous board chair left his position during fall 2015 because of disagreement with the minister.

During spring 2016, Ms Wærsted was appointed new board chair. She had until then been president for Nordea's Norway subsidiary, and she had considerable board experience. Nordea is the largest bank in Scandinavian. Her finance background contrasted with that of the entrepreneurial Mr Brekke. Their political backgrounds were highlighted in the media during the fall 2016 conflict. The chair had been appointed by the conservative minister Ms Mæland, while the CEO had top positions in the Norwegian Social Democratic Party, including state secretary in the Ministry of Defence from 1993 to 1996.

During the fall of 2016, the board of directors of the Telenor Group consisted of eleven members in addition to the chair (Ms Wærsted). Employees elected three of the eleven. Of the five women board members, four, all shareholder elected, lived outside Norway (i.e. London and Switzerland). Four of the board members, the chair included, were elected during spring 2016.

The two main criticisms against Mr Brekke as CEO were that incorrect information was given in his CV about his undergraduate grades and that Telenor in Asia had acted in a corrupt way. A main example was that Telenor's mobile phone company in Bangladesh had sponsored and as a result received help from the special forces in the local police. Voices in the press were also critical of his earlier participation in the Social Democratic Party. The main criticism in the press against Ms Wærsted was that she had overstepped her position in attempting to remove the CEO without a formal board decision.

The Telenor story illustrates the importance of understanding actors, their motivations and interactions. The story shows various points about micro strategizing, and about how micro meets macro. First, in most countries the board is formally a collegiate decision-making body with the power of hiring and firing the CEO. This is not the charge of the chair alone. Formal regulations need to be followed. Second, the case shows the importance of power and influence in different arenas, including political and international influences. Third, it highlights the importance of habitus and different forms of capital, social identities and identifications, including gender, ideologies and the balance between governance and entrepreneurial identities. Fourth, boardroom dynamics and processes must be understood. If the board members had supported the chair, they would at the same time have had to criticize themselves and conclude that they had been doing an insufficient or even bad job when recruiting Mr Brekke as CEO and president. All the arguments behind the criticism of Mr Brekke should have been known before he was appointed. A board will in addition normally allow a new CEO to have a 'honeymoon period'.

As Ms Wærsted remained board chair, we may see the next part of the story when the minister of industry and fishery, Ms Mæland, replaces board members, and thus she may open the gate for replacing Mr Brekke.

3.4.3 Actors: Resources and Types of Capital (Sociology)

How can we describe our resources, and how can they be used in the board setting? I have recently been fascinated by Bourdieu's contributions.[20] He argues that we have different types of resources or capital that go far beyond economic capital. He argues for economic, social, cultural and symbolic capital. Economic capital may facilitate the development of other types of capital. Social capital is developed through social relations and networks. Important concepts include reciprocity, trust and cooperation. Social capital includes both tangible and intangible resources and how they interact. Cultural capital refers to our social assets that may promote our social mobility. It contains the material and

---

[20] See Bourdieu 1977 or Lizardo 2004.

symbolic goods a society considers rare and important. Cultural capital is often related to the habitus concept. Habitus is about embodied dispositions that organize the way we perceive the social world. The Telenor case exemplified this. These dispositions are usually shared by people with similar backgrounds. Habitus represents the way a group culture or personal history may form our social actions and us as individuals. Symbolic capital includes resources available to us on the basis of our honour, prestige or recognition and is earned on an individual basis.

3.4.4   Actors: Cognition and Identities (Social Psychology)

Behavioural perspectives of boards and of the human side of corporate governance focus on people as core actors and use micro-level approaches. These include cognitions and the motivation of the core actors. The cognitive aspect includes how our language helps us identify and analyze reality. However, our language is not static. It can develop, and this development is often a result of what we learn or think. Do I see a business from a finance or from an entrepreneurial perspective? Do I focus on legal requirements and compliance, or do I focus on technical solutions? We need to identify which lenses we are using, and to be conscious about problems and possibilities that are related to cognition and the different lenses.

Identities may also shape behaviour. We need to be aware of the identity, social identity and identifications of the actors (Huse et al. 2011: 12–13; Melkumov et al. 2015). Identity theory focuses on our roles and help us understand what is driving us – and in which direction. Social identity theory focuses on how social categories help define who we are. Identification represents the importance of an identity. I argued in the Telenor case that not only differences in education but also the identities, social identities and identifications contributed to explaining the behaviours.

3.4.5   Actors: Motivation and Preferences (Psychology)

Lessons from psychology have often been overlooked in studies about boards of directors. In recent studies, we have tried to explore aspects of group dynamics, stereotyping, biases and how men and women may differ, but the psychology literature also contributes significantly in helping us understand the motivations and preferences of existing and potential board members. However, I wonder why lessons from psychology are not included in understanding boards of directors. My immediate reaction was why we do not discuss Abraham Maslow in relation to corporate governance and the selection of board members. What is the relationship between board positions and Maslow's pyramid of needs? Much of the discussion seems to be about money and status. Self-determination theory (Deci & Ryan 2010) is concerned with supporting our natural or intrinsic tendencies to behave in a sound way. It has made a contribution in this debate as it conceptualizes motivation in a continuum from non-internalized to internalized, and the theory explicitly acknowledges that different types of motivations may occur simultaneously. The territory for self-determination theory is in the interplay between the extrinsic forces and intrinsic motives.

I am presently working with various colleagues in applying sociology and psychology to explore issues in the discussion about women on boards.[21] One of these projects is about what Juliane Göke labels the 'academic housewife'.[22] In the current debate about advancing women's careers, it is often assumed that all women as well as all men have career ambitions; but what is a career, and is it true that we all aspire for careers? And how is career related to power? A career, however, can be achieved outside the workplace, and power can be other than that from a formal corporate position. Social careers for women have traditionally been achieved through upward marriages, and power may

---

[21] Cathrine Seierstad helps me apply sociological perspectives on questions related to the Norwegian golden skirts, Hannah Möltner with applying psychology in understanding leakages in the corporate talent pipeline and Alessandro Rigolini on the importance of social and relational capital for women and power in Italy.

[22] Juliane Göke is one of my PhD students, and her PhD work is on understanding leakages in the corporate career pipeline.

be exercised by influencing and educating, for example, in the family setting.[23]

More men than women still prefer to follow the corporate career track. The core of Hakim's preference theory (Hakim 2000) is that some women make deliberate choices to pursue careers in the workplace, and some women make deliberate choices not to pursue workplace careers and the remaining group of women are balancing motivations of workplace careers and other possibilities.[24] These choices are not directly related to talents or possibilities, but to preferences. Hakim argues that similar preferences may exist for men, but the distribution is different. However, possibilities, values, preferences and perceptions of power vary significantly across countries.[25] Women may in some countries have significant presence and power on the political arena, while women's corporate power may be focused more in other places.

3.4.6 Summary and Conclusions

We need to identify and understand core actors, their motivations and their interactions. It is insufficient to assume that everybody wants to become a board member or pursue business careers. We need to approach and understand the motivations and possibilities of individual actors, both men and women. Life is more than a corporate career, power and money. Self-realization, philanthropic and altruistic choices should also be appreciated. Giving men the freedom to leave the corporate pipeline may be one way to achieving a culture of appreciating gender equality.

My motto 'Life is too short to drink bad wine' includes two main aspects. The first is related to motivation: life is too short to spend on issues or activities that are not important. Other things are important besides a corporate career. The other aspect is energy. I spend time with people who give me energy rather than take away energy, people who attract and stimulate me.

---

[23] See e.g. Hakim 2000: chap. 6.   [24] See Hakim 2000: table 6:1 .
[25] My cross-country observations about motivations and backgrounds for women becoming board members are presented in Huse 2018.

Giving and receiving energy depends on individual people, and how they interact. In this setting, we should understand and possibly also appreciate some of the gender-related dynamics existing around boards of directors. More research about the motivation and interactions among core actors is needed.

3.5 Factor 5

Diversity and Women on Boards: The Business Case

I have seen that male members of this board open the envelope in the elevator. We were often joking by saying that the boardroom should be as far as possible away from the garage. The quality of the board meetings was a function of the distance between the boardroom and the garage. (Frøydis in Huse and Solberg 2006: *119).*

Challenges
Our business case studies about women on boards contribute to understanding the importance of diversity and dynamics on boards. Most of the empirical studies behind our findings are from Norway. The proportion of women on boards over the past few years has become one of the major discussion topics in the business press in almost the whole of the Western world, and actors in many countries look to Norway.

When researching business cases with various colleagues, we have focused on behavioural and holistic perspectives, and our findings may be summarized in the following five main points:

- It is important to define value creation outputs and to understand variations in tasks (Huse, Nielsen & Hagen 2009).
- It is important to understand inputs as characteristics of the board members and deep-level diversity (Golden 2017; Huse 2011a; Nielsen & Huse 2010a)
- It is important to understand the moderating factors around how board leadership and structures contribute to using diversity and characteristics of the board members (Huse & Søland 2009; Kanadli, Torchia & Gabaldon 2017).

- It is important to understand processes such as stereotyping, adaptions, preparations and interpersonal and group dynamics (Nielsen & Huse 2010b; Torchia, Calabro & Huse 2011).
- It is important to understand context and contingencies, and that observations may be dynamic (Huse 2011a; Rigolini, Huse & Göke 2017).

Each of the five points represents a challenge to most business case research that is using input-output models, and particularly those leaning on data from public statistics.

Key words: using diversity, leadership, gender-related dynamics, changing the corporate governance debate

3.5.1 Value Creation and Board Tasks

First, who defines value creation and how is value creation defined? There may be differences, for example, between short-term changes in market value on the stock exchange and long-term sustainable value created in the company (Byron & Post 2016; Post & Byron 2015). Societal measures of value creation may also be included, e.g. CSR measures. Some studies observed negative market reactions to the introduction of women on boards in Norway. Some found negative relations between women on boards and financial performance even before the women became board members (Ahern & Dittmar 2012). Second, the impact of women varies with the tasks focused on. Boards may be involved in various value-creating tasks, including, for example, legitimacy, network-ing, advising, strategy development, decision-making, various aspects of control and value distribution. In some studies, we have seen that there may be positive results related to women directors' contributions in strategy, but negative for networking and advisory tasks (Bøhren & Staubo 2016; Huse et al. 2009; Nielsen & Huse 2010b).

3.5.2 Deep-Level Diversity and Characteristics

How are women different from men, and even more important – how are women on boards different from men on boards? It is important to explore deep-level and not only surface-level diversity, and it is important to go beyond biological sex to understand women's contributions. There may be more variations among women than between men and women. Not all women aspiring for board positions have female values (Eagly & Carli 2003), feminine behaviour (Hakim 2011 or a feminist agenda (Gill & Scharff 2013). The women being recruited to boards may have characteristics typically attributed to men (e.g. male values), and they may strongly oppose a feminist agenda. It is thus important to distinguish between characteristics of leaders and characteristics of men and women in general. In one of our studies, we found that the women, on average, were not perceived to have backgrounds different from those of men (general board experience, industry experience and company experience), but those having a different background contributed to creativity in the boardroom (Huse et al. 2009). Board members elected by the employees bring more diversity than the women do.[26] 'Golden skirts' is the label applied to women who make a living by belonging to many boards (Huse 2011a; Seierstad & Opsahl 2011). I distinguish four categories of golden skirts (Huse 2011a): (a) the young, smart and clever; (b) the ambitious and pragmatic; (c) the iron fists; and (d) the business experienced. They all had different backgrounds and motivations, and they contributed differently to board tasks and value creation.

3.5.3 Board Leadership and the Use of Diversity

Good board leadership and good board structures can influence the level of diversity, and board leadership and structures may thus moderate the impact of diversity on performance (Huse & Søland 2009). Boards are often set up for fast decision-making and the knowledge and skills of board members are rarely fully utilized (Forbes & Milliken 1999). The team leadership role of the chair thus becomes particularly important. The use of the knowledge

---

[26] In Huse et al. 2009 we used a Norwegian sample. Board members in Norway are elected either by the shareholder or by the employees. The women may be elected by either category.

and skills of the women on boards will highly depend on the board chair and the chair's leadership style and attitudes (Kanadli et al. 2017). Leadership may also include aspects of rules and norms, e.g. board developmental activities and evaluations.

3.5.4 Board Processes

First, gender role stereotyping: the impact of women on boards depends on how they are perceived by other board members. A male in-group board may reduce the impact of the women, if women are excluded or just considered as tokens. In one study (Nielsen & Huse 2010b), we applied stereotyped trait and equality perception theories, and found that when women directors have different professional experiences than the men on the board, this may create significant barriers for women to influence board decisions. Recruiting women with nontraditional backgrounds to boards may reduce their ability to influence board decisions. Goldeng (2017) found that from a power perspective, women with limited experiences within the actual company, from other boards and from business in general would have fewer possibilities to influence board decision-making. However, the power or influence will change when women get more experience in these areas.

Second, critical mass: the impact of women on boards depends on whether the women are adapting to an existing board culture. The critical mass theory implies that an out-group will need to have a critical mass to influence decision-making. Kanter (1976) argued that there is a need for a critical mass of women to influence decision-making in male-dominated groups. In the context of women on boards, it has been argued that the critical mass is three women. When only one or two women are on a board, they will not be able to challenge the existing board culture. This is supported in some of our studies. We found that it is important to have at least three women on a board to increase the specific contributions of the women. Torchia et al. (2011) show support for the critical mass arguments in relation to board strategic tasks and organizational innovation.

Third, tokenism: selecting women on boards may be a result of external pressure taking several forms. It may be from mild to very strong and urgent. Rigolini et al. (2017) distinguished three types of pressures: gentle(-men) pressure (mild), voluntary action pressure (strong, but not urgent) and quota pressure (strong and urgent). We found in an Italian sample that the characteristics of women appointed to boards varied depending on the existing pressure for adding women to boards. Furthermore, women may be seen as tokens to meet such external pressures. We observed that women may prepare better than men for board meetings (Huse & Solberg 2006), particularly when they see themselves as tokens. Awareness about possible tokenism increases competence and preparation.

Fourth, gender-related dynamics: things may change when women and men are together. The behaviour of men and the atmosphere in the board often changes when a woman is present. Several of our studies showed that there may be a better atmosphere in boardrooms with some women than in those without women. The atmosphere becomes more caring and listening. A positive atmosphere and boardroom climate is often important for attaining cohesiveness and improved board performance (Bilimoria & Huse 1997). However, it is not necessarily the women who directly improve board performance. It may be the men on the boards who start 'baking cakes'. Men may change their behaviour when women are present. Some of our studies have illustrated the existence of various types of gender-related dynamics (e.g. Huse & Solberg 2006). Flirtatious behaviour may take place, not necessarily only during the board meetings. Women may have different types of relational capital than men (Hakim 2011), and some men may, because of this dynamic, volunteer to mentor or sponsor women.

3.5.5 Context and Contingencies

There may be learning effects on individual, group, organizational and societal levels. Most business case studies are static, but effects may in reality change over time and place. Reactions to women on boards may be different when it is rare to have women on boards compared to when it is normal and generally accepted (see also Post & Byron 2015). There is also a difference between having women on boards and getting or increasing the number of women on boards. It is not only the characteristics of the women that may change over time and country (Rigolini et al. 2017). Corporate governance definitions and board charges are also changing. In the future, we will see more women with board experience filling the boardrooms. Many of the previously mentioned effects may disappear as it becomes more common to have women on boards. There may even be cross-country lagged learning effects. Furthermore, societal megatrends may affect the business case for women on boards, e.g. the digital transformation of society (Bankewitz et al. 2016). Such changes may include the need for digital knowledge and digital awareness among board members or even more basic needs. The corporate bottleneck focus may be redirected from financial capital to knowledge and communication skills. How will these fast-happening changes affect the business case for women on boards?

3.5.6   Summary and Conclusions

A new understanding of corporate governance is developing. A focus in recent corporate governance debates has been on independent board members who can monitor management. Transparency and value distribution have been the objectives. The discussion about women on boards has led to a focus on competence, diversity and the use of knowledge and skills. Strategic decision-making and long-term sustainable value creation have become the objectives. This argument is illustrated in the Table 2.[27]

Important aspects of the present international corporate governance debate are on the left-hand side of the table. The core of this debate is found in the financial literature and among actors in the financial markets. Corresponding aspects in the current women on board debates are on the right-hand side. The corresponding concepts reflect opposing positions. This means that the discussion

---

[27] The table is elaborated from Huse 2011a.

Table 2 Corporate governance codes and the women on board debate

Main Focus	The CG Codes Debate and Its Consequences	The Debate about Quotas and about Getting Women on Boards
Characteristics of Boards Members	Independence	Competence
Objectives	Value Distribution	Value Creation
Board Culture	Decision Oriented	Process Oriented
Literature/ Discipline	Finance and Accounting	Entrepreneurship and Leadership
Board Member Identification	Shareholders and Stakeholders	Firm
Time Perspectives	Short	Long
Theory Support	Agency/ Stakeholder	Team Production

about women on boards may redirect the corporate governance debate to focus more on competence, value creation, processes, innovativeness, the strategy literature, firm identification, long termism and team production theory. The business case about the women on board discussion is not only directly related to the contribution of the individual woman. The discussion about women on boards itself may thus change the contribution of boards from control and value distribution to long-term value creation.

3.6 Factor 6

When Micro Meets Macro: Contributing in Actual Discourses

Life is not a problem to be solved, but a reality to be experienced (Søren Kierkegaard[28])

---

[28] Danish philosopher. www.goodreads.com/author/show/6172.S_ren_ Kierkegaard

Challenges

Challenges in this factor include creating a sustainable society, gender equality, gender quotas on boards, understanding golden skirts, the political game and gender discourses. I conclude with a strategic choice perspective. It is possible for individuals like you and me to make an impact. Things do not just happen by themselves. We can make a change. The presentation of this factor follows this outline: first, the Norwegian story about gender quotas (Hansen & Huse 2011)[29], then discussion of the golden skirts (Huse 2011a), the snowball that started rolling (Machold et al. 2013), institutional complementarities (Iannotta et al. 2016), the political games with actors, motivations and interactions (Seierstad et al. 2017), and finally gender discourses (Huse et al. 2017a, 2017b).

Key words: contribution to society, gender equality, gender quotas on boards, sustainable society, golden skirts, political game, gender discourses, snowball, strategic choice

3.6.1   Getting Women on Boards through Quotas – from a Snowball to an Avalanche

Boards and governance issues must be seen in a larger societal picture. During past years, I have spent considerable efforts on trying to get more women on boards. My attention to gender equality and the discrimination of women started in the late 1970s; ten years later this also became a topic within my research agenda about boards of directors. In Norway's system, board members typically are non-executives (i.e. not members of the company's executive team), and in 1990 only about 4 per cent of the board members of the companies listed on the Oslo Stock Exchange were women. The woman who held the most positions was a shipowner and member of the boards of companies in which she and her family were controlling owners.[30] She even had some board chair positions.

---

[29] I have written about this in many context – often by invitation after a speech. See e.g. Huse 2010, 2012, 2013, 2014 and 2016.

[30] Ms. Annette Olsen in Fred Olsen Shipping.

I here present some reflections about getting women on boards and about quotas. Creating quota legislation is a societal issue, nationally as well as internationally. Quotas may be used for various purposes, including increasing the number of women on boards. Such a quota may have various intended and unintended trickle-down effects – positive as well as negative. However, legal quotas for getting women on boards are clearly not seen as the solution for all gender inequality challenges.

3.6.2 The Norwegian Story

Around 1990, some women attended my classes about boards of directors. Some of them wrote master's theses about the business case for women on boards. Their main interests were getting more women on boards and getting board positions themselves. One of them was particularly successful, and I followed her carefully over some years as a friend and her mentor.[31] During the 1990s, I followed various initiatives in Norway and Sweden to get more women on boards: media argumentations for why this was important, networks, training programs, mentorship programs, development of board-ready women databases, and headhunter initiatives.[32] The focus on getting women on boards was more developed in Sweden than in Norway.[33] One particularly interesting initiative was championed by the Swedish industrialist Carl Bennet and Swedish Minister for Equality Margareta Winberg.[34] In 1999, they suggested that a quota law should be passed. One of the major Swedish banks had already enacted such a quota regulation for all its 135 subsidiary boards. However, as Bennet and Winberg had to bury their quota law suggestion, the ideas were passed over to Norway and Norwegian Equality Minister Valgerd

---

[31] She is one of the four women presented in Bilimoria and Huse (1997).
[32] Huse 2000.
[33] During 1997–2002, I was an adjunct professor at Lunds University and Halmstad University College in Sweden. I was teaching courses about boards of directors, and some of the students wrote their theses about women on boards. From this position, I was able to follow the Swedish initiatives directly.
[34] See e.g. Dagens Industri, 30 August 1999. Newspaper article.

Svarstad Haugland. The snowball started rolling in Norway. During the winter of 2002, only 6 per cent of the board members of public limited companies were women. This was far behind the situation in Sweden. The Norwegian Parliament introduced gender quota regulations for boards of directors in 2003.

The Norwegian gender quota was strongly opposed by the international capital markets, but by spring 2008 the quota regulation was enacted for Norwegian public limited companies. Since then, boards of these companies have averaged about 40 per cent women. Since the introduction of the quota legislation, about 3000 women have gained experience as board members in Norwegian public limited companies.[35] The Norwegian story is told in 'Getting Women on to Corporate Boards: A Snowball Started Rolling in Norway' (Machold et al. 2013).

3.6.3   The Golden Skirts

One of the results of the Norwegian law was that some women made a living from being non-executive board members. These golden skirts received international attention, and by 2008 they had replaced the independent directors of the old boys' network (Huse 2011a). In some of our projects, however, we found that the golden skirts were not a homogeneous group. The women in this group had diverse backgrounds and identities. They hardly knew each other beforehand, were not members on the same boards and their contributions to value-creating boards varied. Some of the women were typically advisors, others were focusing on compliance, some were decision oriented and some focused on creating values in the company in collaboration with the executives. By 2015, the concentration of board memberships of a few golden skirts was reduced (Tørlen 2015).

The main criterion for becoming a board member is having already served as a board member. One result of the Norwegian quota legislation is that many women gained experience as board members.

[35] More than 1800 women were board members during 2007–2010.

3.6.4 A Snowball Has Started Rolling

A snowball started rolling in Norway, and this snowball is becoming a global avalanche (Machold et al. 2013). Political leaders, business leaders, journalists as well as various groups of women from all over the world have closely followed the Norwegian initiatives about a legal quota to achieve gender balance on corporate boards.[36] However, different interests are embedded in distinct and varying ideologies, including various gender codes. Questions are raised about whether and how the Norwegian regulation should be followed in other countries. In this process, I identified a new research project. I wanted to going beyond the surface, to respond to the lessons from Norway.

In this multinational project, we explored and followed core actors and the controlling networks in the debates about women on boards. We observed that the overall international and national corporate governance and board realities might change as a result of these debates. Our arguments were that political and business decision-makers as well as individual actors could receive scientifically based help in formulating their agenda in creating a gender balance policy and a sustainable society. A result may be that boards may move their focus from corporate governance to entrepreneurial perspectives.

The project was designed as a mentorship project where in several countries I actively followed and supported women who wanted to contribute to gender equality through getting more women on boards. The project was positioned as multi-sited ethnography (Marcus 2016). Detailed observations were first made in Italy and in Germany, later in Spain and Slovenia.[37] The snowball

---

[36] I have made more than 100 speeches about lessons from Norway in more than twenty countries. These include speeches in the British, Italian and Slovenian Parliaments, and together with top politicians and cabinet members in Brussels at the EU level, Austria, Germany, Luxembourg, Netherlands, Norway, Scotland, Spain and Sweden.

[37] I was an adjunct professor at various universities in Italy from 2001 to 2012, and a professor from 2012 to 2017 in Germany. During 2015–2016, the mentoring projects were conducted in Spain and Slovenia. See e.g. Izquierdo, Huse and Möltner (2016).

had started rolling, but was the snowball about to grow into an uncontrollable global avalanche?

3.6.5 Institutional Complementarities

In a background project, we studied the existence (Iannotta et al. 2016) of women on boards through institutional complementarities with a configurational approach. We explored consequences of the so-called maternal wall (career challenges caused by motherhood and particularly giving birth, Williams & Segal 2003) and analyzed public policy initiatives and gender labour force participation in twenty-seven European countries (Norway not included). These initiatives included parental leaves, childcare service and forms of regulations to get women on boards. We found evidence of institutional isomorphism and social legitimacy more than rationality, and that effects had to be understood from a complementarity perspective.

In another study (Warner-Søderholm et al. 2017) of twenty-four European countries, we explored the impact of national leadership cultures on getting women on boards. We included multiple macro factors and found that legislation matters.

3.6.6 The Political Game – Where Micro Meets Macro

We learnt about politicking and political games in a study about the role of actors and processes in efforts to get women on boards (Seierstad et al. 2017). We followed the actors and processes in England, Germany, Italy and Norway. Our focus was on learning more about the political games influencing decisions about public policy initiatives to get more women on boards

We looked beyond the institutional setting by focusing on the role of actors. We explored processes that included who the critical actors were that drive and determine these policies, and what motivates them to push for change. The political games, both inside and outside legislative areas, were mapped. These games included the micro politics among various actors and groups of actors in the selected countries.

The contextual landscape has changed since the Norwegian quota was introduced: quotas are no longer a radical concept. Our findings suggest that at a macro level, the countries represent different 'stories' of adopting national public policies to increase women on boards, highly influenced by politicking and the role of actors as well as historical and institutional factors.

This variation suggests that focusing on actors, actor-network theories and analyses may be appropriate and even necessary to apply in future studies about getting women on boards and the use of national public policy initiatives. Similar studies will also be needed to explore more in more depth the dynamics observed. Our observations about key actors, network interactions, motivational factors, national discourses and the different national public policy initiatives imply that national public policy initiatives should not be directly copied from one country to another.

3.6.7 Gender Discourses

In another paper (Huse et al. 2017), we explored underlying gender-related discourses about women's career advancements with a focus on getting women on boards. We used five gender codes to disentangle national gender discourses (Rennison 2012). These are the biological code, meritocracy, the exclusion code, the diversity code and the freedom code.

The codes were coupled with actual discourses in Germany, Italy, Norway, Slovenia and Spain. We used the codes as a sorting frame in our national observations. We found that the national and international discourses about getting women on boards contained many conflicting arguments. The conflicts occurred, for example, within each discourse on a micro level. Those presenting the arguments did not see how the arguments were not aligned and were in conflict. Conflicts also occurred between actors with different backgrounds or those who identified themselves with different codes. However, their arguments were not always coherent with the gender positions they had taken. These actors sometimes avoided communicating their conflicting perspectives, and sometimes they did not understand that their stands in practice conflicted internally. Some of the conflicts related to the understanding of corporate governance frameworks and national board practices, but understandings of conflicting gender codes and identities dominated.

The stereotyped descriptions varied across countries, and many arguments could not directly be transferred from one country to another. Some discourses for getting women on boards may be positive, while others may be destructive. Whether they are positive or negative is not directly related to the various dominating gender codes, but to how the codes are coupled.

The gender codes can be coupled in various ways (Rennisson 2012: 246–49). They may go beyond comfortable blindness, contradictory controversies, creative misunderstandings and cynic parasitism. They may also lead to complementary mutualism and constructive alliances. On the other hand, the lack of a joint discourse limits the possibilities for joint efforts for advancing women's career possibilities. Stereotypes only representing parts of the reality are used in the arguments for promoting women, and these arguments may easily be contradicted and thus be obstacles for sustainable progress. Comfortable blindness is when the codes are living in separate rooms next to each other; contradictory controversy occurs when the representatives of the different codes are in implacable conflicts; creative misunderstanding takes place when there is a one-sided exploitation of the other's arguments to support one's own; and cynic parasitism refers to when one code infects the logic of another. Complementary mutualism takes place when both stands benefit from the presence of the other, while constructive alliances occur when a pattern is observed and connections are made across the various codes (Rennisson 2012: 246–49)

3.6.8　Summary and Conclusions

The effects of quota regulations depend on the contexts and actors. We must also understand the underlying dynamics related to individuals, groups/boards, organizations/corporations and society (national and international). Our concluding observation is that the discourses and their outcomes can be moderated or changed. This means that we still have the possibility of influencing the direction of the snowball that has started rolling. We can also impact its consequences.

Societies are composed of individuals, and individuals are not living in vacuums. Life is not a problem to be solved individually, but together we can challenge the reality also beyond ourselves.

4 The Development of a Research Stream

Life is too short to drink bad wine. (Johan Wolfgang von Goethe)

The arena for boards and corporate governance has not been static during the past decade, and developments have escalated. In BGV, I tried to accumulate knowledge about boards of directors with a focus on behavioural perspectives. The lessons from BGV have been developed and disseminated through the Norefjell workshops and the Norefjell group. Here I present the research stream that has been evolving from these workshops. I will finally also bring some attention to the research philosophy behind my contributions.

From 2010 to 2012, I was president of the European Academy of Management (EURAM), and from 2012 to 2017 I had a late career professorship at Witten/Herdecke University in Germany.[38] The EURAM presidency helped me fine-tune an agenda on positive organizational scholarship and contribute to the development of a European-based community of engaged management scholars. This period not only introduced me to the importance of doing impactful research. I was also fortunate to be able to sense motions in academic associations from all over the world. The challenges of having English as la lingua franca also became

---

[38] From 2012 to 2015, I held the Reinhard-Mohn-Stiftungslehrstuhl für Unternehmensführung, Wirtschaftsethik und gesellshaftlichen Wandel (Reinhard Mohn Endowment Chair of Management, Business Ethics and Societal Change). Reinhard Mohn was the entrepreneur who developed the Bertelsmann corporation. His philosophy was to develop business and society by developing people and the organizational culture.

evident. Witten/Herdecke University is a small German private elite university founded on anthroposophical values that reflect people-oriented, reflective and holistic approaches. The students are learning to use both brain and heart, business disciplines are integrated with other disciplines, long-term societal values are integrated with sustainable business values and the teaching is based on discussion and reflection. I was also fortunate to work with, mentor and be influenced by many PhD students and junior faculty. This period has strengthened the focus on evaluating my research on its contribution to social and societal change and development.

4.1   Boards and Wine: Developing a Toolbox

The corporate governance toolbox has for a long time mainly contained four tools, and one main objective influences the development or maintenance of good board behaviour (Finkelstein & Mooney 2003). The objective for boards has been to monitor corporate financial performance. The main tools have been the number of board members, the insider/outsider ratio, that the CEO and the board chair is the same person (CEO duality) and the shareholding of board members.

I like to bring my glass of wine when making executive presentations about boards of director. Wine may make many contributions, and my vocabulary about wine goes far beyond its colour or its price. It goes beyond the grapes being used, the country the wine is produced in and the *terroir* where it is made. I also know that wine is about people and relates to the characteristics of the producer, the production methods, the harvest and the vintage. It is about the pairing of wine with food, the place and the people I am with when enjoying the wine, and my own mood. It is about wine diseases, the storing of the wine and the temperature of the wine when drinking. The wine vocabulary is much bigger than the vocabulary we apply when developing boards and corporate governance systems. Is that because wine is more important than corporate governance?

BGV contributed to developing and systematizing a language about boards and corporate governance. It contributes to sorting out nuances and differences between subjects and objects, and between substantives and verbs in the corporate governance debate and development. My contribution may possibly be as a concept-developing scholar: to observe and reflect on practice, and to employ and refine words and concepts being observed. The contribution also includes sorting the various concepts and observations, and creating sentences that are meaningful. This is about developing the toolbox, and it is about developing those who will use the toolbox.

It is also about challenging the lamp and hammer syndrome (Huse 1998: 218–19). The lamp and hammer syndrome is about research convenience and opportunism. We should not only do research on issues that relate to the usual suspects and corporate financial performance. We should not only do research on topics where variables are easily identifiable, or only use methods we already know and that are generally accepted. We need to put our efforts on issues of importance for the present and even more for the future. This is not always easy but is still what we need to aim for. Studying behaviour and processes is not straightforward. There may be a need for exploiting theories and methods in research about boards and corporate governance that are not common, which the Norefjell workshops consider.

4.2 Lenses and Perspectives

A research stream is an accumulation of knowledge. Research is not conducted in a vacuum. Good research builds on the knowledge from the past, and it has consequences for the future. Many streams of research about corporate governance in general and about boards of directors in particular exist. What makes different streams of research similar or distinct from each other is often a result of communication, but it is also about values. It is thus important to understand the roots of our research.

We may use the lenses or glasses metaphor to show the importance of understanding differences. I have my reading glasses, computer glasses, driving glasses, gallery glasses, 3D glasses and different types of sunglasses. My observations and my perception of reality changes depending on which glasses I am using. When using my finance glasses, I define corporate governance from the perspective of investors or owners, and corporate governance is then often the same as governance by owners. When I use my accounting or law glasses, the corporate governance definition easily becomes close to 'comply or explain' or 'box-ticking'. When I am using my strategy and management glasses, I use a corporate governance definition related to value creation in the company. In BGV, I used the following definition of corporate governance: 'Corporate Governance is seen as the interactions between various internal and external actors and the board members in directing a firm for value creation' (Huse 2007: 15). This definition is a triangulation definition built on the work of Monks and Minow (1995).[39] It has its focus on and emphasizes behavioural perspectives and the human side through the attributes and interactions of various actors (Ees et al. 2009). The definition applies an objective in line with the core strategy literature (see e.g. Barney 1991; Porter 1995).

4.3 Building Blocks

Several streams of corporate governance research relate to boards of directors. BGV and the Norefjell workshops are positioned in the interface of the core strategy and organizational behaviour literature. However, there are contributions from political economy, regulations and socio-economics (e.g. Aguilera et al. 2008; Aguilera & Jackson 2010; Blair 1995; Blair & Stout 1999, 2001; Clarke 2004; Clarke & Clegg 2000; Terjesen et al. 2015); the theory

---

[39] Monks and Minow (1995) identify the shareholders, the managers and the board members as the most important actors, but various other actors are also identified. In later versions of their textbook, they are not so specific on definitions.

of the firm (see e.g. Felin, Foss & Ployhart 2015; Foss, Husted & Michailova 2010; Foss & Lindenberg 2013; Grandori 2004; Osterloh & Frey 2000; Osterloh, Frey & Frost 2001); international business (e.g. Filatotchev et al. 2007; Thomsen & Pedersen 2000; Oxelheim et al. 2013; Wright et al. 2005); agency theory and executive compensation (e.g. Berrone & Gomez-Mejia 2009); comparative corporate governance (e.g. Clarke 2007;Mallin 2011); and class hegemony and elites (e.g. Davis 2009a, 2009b); venture capital; and various streams about family firm governance, stewardship and stakeholder approaches, public sector governance and boards in public management and also various stream of finance-inspired input-output studies. This list does not include contributions from streams in other disciplines, including law, accounting and finance.

Several cornerstones and building blocks have been leading to the value-creating board framework presented in BGV. In Huse (2009a) I presented the following building blocks:

- Mace 1971: Mace presented the gap between myths and reality and showed realities behind the managerial hegemony.
- Fama and Jensen 1983a: Fama and Jensen presented how boards could be used in an agency theory framework.
- Zahra and Pearce 1989: Zahra and Pearce illustrated the need to study board effectiveness and value creation in intermediate steps, and how board performance may be understood differently depending on the theoretical underpinning.
- Pettigrew 1992: Pettigrew emphasized the need to explore boards as open systems, integrating sociology and leadership.
- Forbes and Milliken 1999: Forbes and Milliken presented boards as decision-making groups.

The value-creating board research framework, as used in BGV, is a summary of these cornerstones.

Other important building blocks for the value-creating board framework came from Andrews (1981), who considered boards' strategy involvement; Kosnik (1987), who contrasted agency theory and managerial hegemony; Baysinger and Hoskisson (1990), who specified the need to be precise when referring to various boards tasks; Johnson, Daily and Ellstrand (1996), who argued for the death of black box studies; and Blair and Stout (1999), who introduced team production theory. In addition, there were contributions from resource dependence theory, the resource-based view, stewardship theory, stakeholder theory, and several seminal articles by Davis, Hambrick, Ocasio, Westphal, Zajac and others.

This research framework proposed a research agenda behind the development of the value-creating board research survey instrument. Working with this instrument was glue for scholars in the development of the Norefjell group.

4.4 *The Value-creating Board Survey and the Norefjell Workshops*

The Norefjell research stream on behavioural perspectives about value-creating boards is today strongly influenced by BGV, the value-creating board survey instrument (Huse 2009c; Sellevoll, Huse & Hansen 2007), and my EURAM and Witten/Herdecke experiences.

The first version of the value-creating board framework was presented in 2002.[40] It was used in fine-tuning the value-creating research project and survey instrument, and the first version of the instrument was launched after several pilot studies, during the fall of 2003.[41] Scholars from various European countries came together during the winter of 2004 to explore how this instrument could be scrutinized outside Norway. They met in Oslo and at Norefjell.

The Norefjell Board Governance International Research Workshops on Behavioural Perspectives of Boards have been held every year since 2004. On average, about twenty-five PhD

---

[40] As a paper at the Corporate Governance Conference celebrating the 100 years of Bocconi University, November 2002.

[41] The Research Council of Norway financed the main project (2003–2007), and various actors in Norwegian industry supported it. The project developed through several studies during the 1990s, and a pilot study testing the survey instrument was conducted in 2000–2001.

students and faculty from a large number of countries participate each year. During these workshops, we discuss and explore ways to research and understand behavioural perspectives of boards of directors. These workshops have been the cornerstone in developing a distinct international research stream about boards of directors (Gabrielsson et al. 2014; Huse 2009a).

What makes this research stream distinct? The framework combines observations of actual board behaviour with theoretical reflections, and it is a result of an abductive approach. I define 'abductive' as taking a best shot by going back and forth between inductive and deductive approaches. The cornerstones and building blocks presented earlier were studied through several deductive as well as inductive projects about actual board behaviour (see e.g. Huse 2009a). The stream has links to a US-based management strategy tradition with deductive approaches, as well as to European and Australian/New Zealand traditions that are leaning on inductive approaches. A particular feature is the attention on processes and actual behaviour used within the boardroom, and that board performance and effectiveness are measured in intermediate steps.

Most of the empirical studies have been performed in Europe with European data. This has also shaped the stream:

- First, in Europe there is an awareness of variations in corporate governance systems and board accountability.
- Second, within national European settings, most firms are considered to be small or medium size compared to the Fortune 500 companies that are used in many US-based studies.
- Third, the tenure track system for faculty in Europe was not as developed as that in the United States from the 1980s to the 2000s. That made it possible to do research with longer time horizons, including the possibility to collect primary data.
- Fourth, scholars in Europe review research and research traditions published in various languages and also in other outlets than what are common in the United States. This also contributes to more venturesome and diverse research designs.

This stream 'brings together behavioural, institutional, entrepreneurial and ethical approaches to the study of boards and governance' (Gabrielsson et al. 2014: 117): 'The research conducted spans legal and political debates on corporate governance at the macro level to micro level behaviour inside and outside the boardroom and relates to a variety and countries and contexts' (Gabrielsson et al. 2014: 117). There has been a core reasoning at the Norefjell workshops that research must be relevant and have its impact on business. The stream focuses on the behavioural perspectives that should be used and the belief that there are better ways of measuring processes than through proxies. Research has also been evaluated based on how it communicates with board members in small- and medium-sized companies.

The value-creating board survey instrument exists in two main editions, and they have been used in various countries. The second edition was developed based on lessons learnt from the first edition. General scales were changed from five points to seven points, and items and variables were revised and developed based on empirical experiences and statistical analyses. For example, the items suggested by Forbes and Milliken (1999) were used directly in the first edition, but they were revised in the second based on empirical validation and experiences. Similar changes were made to the formulations in the first edition suggested directly by Amy Hillman and James Westphal.

Versions of the first edition have been used in the Netherlands, Belgium, Italy and Norway. Versions of the second edition have been used in Norway, Turkey, Denmark and Finland. Versions of the instrument have also been used in other countries as its design and questions have been openly available to scholars.

The Norefjell workshop has been an important outlet for discussing and disseminating research on behavioural perspectives on boards and governance. International journals such as *Corporate Governance: An International Review, British Journal of Management* and *Journal of Business Ethics* publish many articles from this stream, but these articles also appear in several US-based journals, for example, *Journal of Management* and *Journal of*

Organizational Behavior. The most cited contributions have focus on 'opening the black box' (Zona & Zattoni 2007), board task involvement (Huse et al. 2009; Minichilli, Zattoni & Zona 2009; Minichilli et al. 2012; Pugliese & Wenstøp 2007), board decision-making culture (Zattoni, Gnan & Huse 2015), women on boards (Nielsen & Huse 2010a, 2010b) and board leadership (Gabrielsson et al. 2007; Machold et al. 2011). Board task involvement and innovation (Torchia et al. 2011) have often been used as independent variables. Several studies have explored boards in SMEs, family firms and entrepreneurial firms as well as for international comparisons.

4.5 Recent Developments and Suggestions for Further Research

Recent studies about women on boards have taken this stream of research further. Several studies have been applying different types of interviews, and various types of participant observation studies have been developed. These studies have incorporated additional sets of theories, including gender and diversity theories, and the objectives have moved beyond exploring the business utility case to also relating to societal and justice arguments. Comparisons across counties have been conducted. During the past decade, a tremendous debate and resulting change have taken place in academic attention, but even more in practice about having more women on boards. This discussion has showed many aspects of board dynamics. Such dynamics occurs in the boardroom, but also outside and in the society.

Topics presented at the Norefjell workshop in 2017 are listed in Figure 3. The figure is a contribution to a research jigsaw about boards, governance and value creation. It contains two separate, but overlapping topics, namely, value-creating board studies and women on board studies. The numbers indicate the factors that are reflected the most in the actual group of topics.

The topics and studies about value-creating boards and women on boards are in general separate, but there are several common

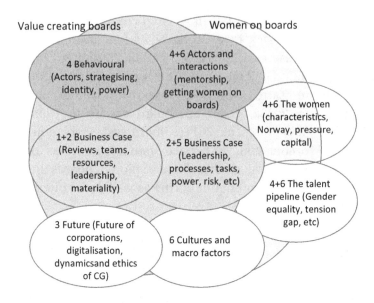

Figure 3 A research jigsaw about boards, governance and value creation

denominators. The figure also shows that the women on board studies introduce and focus on various aspects of boards, governance and value creation that have not been explored or exploited in existing value-creating board studies. Issues related to the dynamics of human capital on boards, preferences and motivation, gender dynamics and national cultures are being studied. The value-creating board studies are now attempting to include consequences of the digital transformation of society.

The value-creating board research studies at the Norefjell workshops have included the following:

- Studies about the business case are focusing on creating sustainable firm-level value creation, cognition, teams, resources, leadership and materiality. These are meso-level studies where the board is most often the unit of analysis. The empirical studies in this group are often leaning on surveys and psychometric analyses, but also on interviews. Some of the core concepts being used are dynamic capabilities, absorptive capacity, ambidexterity and decision-making theories. Input-process-output models with various moderating effects are being used. Reviews of board tasks and board performance are also being conducted, and the application of team production theory is being explored. The characteristics of a grand theory (see Factor 1), values and the value chain (see Factor 2) are reflected here.

• The second group includes studies of behavioural dynamics with the focus on actors, interactions, identities, power and strategizing. These are the micro-level studies. The empirical studies are leaning on direct observations as 'flies on the wall' or 'one of the lads', but also on interviews. Narratives and discourse analyses have been applied. Behavioural theory and strategy as practice approaches are being used in this group. The factor of understanding actors and dynamics (see Factor 4) is reflected here.

• The future of corporations, digitalization and sustainable societal values are the core in the macro-level studies. These issues are reflected in the factor about preparing for the future (see Factor 3). Moral reasoning and value-based arguments are important. These studies are looking at think tanks and scenarios, but also case studies, cross national comparisons and surveys. We explore consequences of public policy initiatives, but also the contributions of individual actors. Approaches about social change and strategic choice are being applied, but also reflections about maladaptions and unintended consequences.

The women on board research agendas are sorted in five main groups:

• The business case approaches of women on boards are similar to those in the value-creating board group but focus more on diversity, stereotypes and processes. These studies include aspects of power, risk taking and the importance of board leadership and structures. These business case studies focus the importance of understanding time and space. They are reflected in the factor about diversity and the business case for women on boards (see Factor 5).

- The second group of women on board studies is similar to the behavioural dynamics and micro-level approaches in the value-creating board agenda. The women on board studies have a stronger focus on societal, public policy and international actors. The focus is on the micro level, but these studies also involve macro-level consequences. Such perspectives are presented in the factor relating to micro meeting macro (see Factor 6). Cross-country comparisons are used.
- Several studies about women on boards contain cross-national comparisons of macro factors. The objective with such studies is often to meet needs about gender equality in society. Such studies are also in our portfolio and are reflected in the factor of preparing for the future (see Factor 3). The focus is on institutional theories, the existence and use of public policy instruments and national and regional cultures, including the use of GLOBE data (House et al. 2004).
- A fourth group of our women on board studies concerns exploring characteristics of existing and potential board members – both women and men. Here we lean on concepts and perspectives from Bourdieu about different types of capital and of habitus (see Factor 4). Interviews and various sources for descriptions of individuals are uses, e.g. including information from the Internet. Comparisons are made between men and women, among men and women, and across and within countries and regions. Lessons from this group of studies are also combined with lessons from the groups presented earlier.
- The final group of studies is about leakages in the talent pipeline, career advancement, feminism and gender codes. These studies are mainly reflected in the factors about actors (see Factor 4) and contributions in actual discourses (see Factor 6).

4.6 And the Moral Is . . .

The secret behind BGV and its contributions may be the Norefjell group. The Norefjell group and the Norefjell workshops do not only challenge existing research about boards and governance. This stream of research approaches a new way or paradigm of doing research. It is not only because it focuses on values, sustainability, actors, dynamics and venturesome methods. Lessons from the evolution of this stream are questioning dominating paradigms of publications as the key performance indicator, and it is questioning individual research credits. The previously presented Goethe citation that 'Life is too short to drink bad wine' has become one of my personal mottoes. It reminds me that I need to make strict priorities and use my efforts on what is most important. This I need to do together with people who give me energy. The key performance indicator should be that our research is important for future generations, and that the contributions are not a result of individual efforts. The contributions from the Norefjell group are the result of an open innovation approach and a sharing research philosophy. Scholars and students have met in the Norefjell network, and they have freely shared their knowledge and experiences. This stream is about learning together. It is about taking the risk that somebody will steal your ideas and thus get credit for them. Open innovation is about a continuous learning and sharing process. Journal publication will not be the most important, but that of conducting important and meaningful research together with a group of engaged management scholars.

References

Åberg, C. (2017). *Dynamic Managerial Capabilities and Boards of Directors.* PhD thesis Witten/Herdecke University.

Åberg, C., Kazemargi, N. & Bankewitz, M. (2017). Strategists on the Board in a Digital Era. *Business and Management Research, 6*(2), 40.

Åberg, C., Bankewitz, M., Knockaert, M. & Huse, M. (2017). Service Tasks of Boards of Directors: A Critical Literature Review and Research Agenda. Presentation Academy of Management Meeting, Atlanta.

Aguilera, R. V., Filatotchev, I., Gospel, H. & Jackson, G. (2008). An Organizational Approach to Comparative Corporate Governance: Costs, Contingencies, and Complementarities. *Organization Science, 19*(3), 475–492.

Aguilera, R. V., & Jackson, G. (2010). Comparative and International Corporate Governance. *Academy of Management Annals, 4*(1), 485–556.

Ahern, K. R., & Dittmar, A. K. (2012). The Changing of the Boards: The Impact on Firm Valuation of Mandated Female Board Representation. *The Quarterly Journal of Economics, 127*(1), 137–197.

Alchian, A. A., & Demsetz, H. (1972). Production, Information Costs, and Economic Organization. *The American Economic Review, 62*(5), 777–795.

Andrews, K. R. (1981). Corporate Strategy as a Vital Function of the Board. *Harvard Business Review, 59*(6), 174–184.

Aoki, M. (1984). *The Co-operative Game Theory of the Firm.* Oxford University Press.

Ashforth, B. E., & Mael, F. (1989). Social Identity Theory and the Organization. *Academy of Management Review, 14*(1), 20–39.

Bammens, Y., Voordeckers, W. & Van Gils, A. (2011). Boards of Directors in Family Businesses: A Literature Review and Research Agenda. *International Journal of Management Reviews, 13*(2), 134–152.

Bankewitz, M., Åberg, C. & Teuchert, C. (2016). Digitalization and Boards of Directors: A New Era of Corporate Governance? *Business and Management Research, 5*(2), 58.

Barnett, J., & O'Neill, S. (2010). Maladaptation. *Global Environmental Change*, 20, 211–213.

Barney, J. (1991). Firm Resources and Sustained Competitive Advantage. *Journal of Management*, 17(1), 99–120.

Baysinger, B., & Hoskisson, R. E. (1990). The Composition of Boards of Directors and Strategic Control: Effects on Corporate Strategy. *Academy of Management Review*, 15(1), 72–87.

Berrone, P., & Gomez-Mejia, L. R. (2009). Environmental Performance and Executive Compensation: An Integrated Agency-institutional Perspective. *Academy of Management Journal*, 52(1), 103–126.

Bilimoria, D., & Huse, M. (1997). A Qualitative Comparison of the Boardroom Experiences of US and Norwegian Women Corporate Directors. *International Review of Women and Leadership*, 3(2), 63–76.

Blair, M. M. (1995). *Ownership and Control: Rethinking Corporate Governance for the 21st Century*. Brookings Institution.

Blair, M. M., & Stout, L. A. (1999). A Team Production Theory of Corporate Law. *Virginia Law Review*, 85(2), 247–328.

Blair, M. M., & Stout, L. A. (2001). Trust, Trustworthiness, and the Behavioral Foundations of Corporate Law. *University of Pennsylvania Law Review*, 149(6), 1735–1810.

Bøhren, Ø., & Staubo, S. (2016). Mandatory Gender Balance and Board Independence. *European Financial Management*, 22(1), 3–30.

Boivie, S., Bednar, M. K., Aguilera, R. V. & Andrus, J. L. (2016). Are Boards Designed to Fail? The Implausibility of Effective Board Monitoring. *The Academy of Management Annals*, 10(1), 319–407.

Bourdieu, P. (1977). Outline of a Theory of Practice. Cambridge University Press.

Byron, K., & Post, C. (2016). Women on Boards of Directors and Corporate Social Performance: A Meta-Analysis. *Corporate Governance: An International Review*, 24(4), 428–442.

Catalyst (2014). *Women CEOs of the Fortune 1000*. Catalyst.

Charan, R., Carey, D. & Useem, M. (2014). *Boards That Lead. When to Take Charge, When to Partner, and When to Stay Out of the Way*. Harvard Business Review Press.

Clarke, T. (ed.). (2004). *Theories of Corporate Governance: The Philosophical Foundations of Corporate Governance*. Routledge.

Clarke, T. (2007). *International Corporate Governance: A Comparative Approach*. Routledge.

Clarke, T., & Clegg, S. (2000). Management Paradigms for the New Millennium. *International Journal of Management Reviews, 2*(1), 45–64.

Cyert, R. M., & March, J. G. (1963). A Behavioral Theory of the Firm. Prentice Hall.

Daily, C. M., Dalton, D. R. & Cannella, A. A. (2003). Corporate Governance: Decades of Dialogue and Data. *Academy of Management Review, 28*(3), 371–382.

Dalton, D. R., & Dalton, C. M. (2011). Integration of Micro and Macro Studies in Governance Research: CEO Duality, Board Composition, and Financial Performance. *Journal of Management, 37*(2), 404–411

Davis, J. H., Schoorman, F. D. & Donaldson, L. (1997). Toward a Stewardship Theory of Management. *Academy of Management Review, 22*(1), 20–47.

Davis, G. F. (2009a). *Managed by the Markets: How Finance Re-Shaped America.* Oxford University Press.

Davis, G. F. (2009b). The Rise and Fall of Finance and the End of the Society of Organizations. *The Academy of Management Perspectives, 23*(3), 27–44.

Davis, G. F. (2013). After the Corporation. *Politics & Society, 41*(2), 283–308.

Davis, G. F., & Cobb, J. A. (2010). Corporations and Economic Inequality around the World: The Paradox of Hierarchy. *Research in Organizational Behavior, 30*, 35–53.

Deci, E. L., & Ryan, R. M. (2010). *Self-Determination.* John Wiley & Sons, Inc.

Directors and Boards. (2014) Is Your Company's Board of Directors Creating Value – or Destroying It? *Directors and Boards Magazine, 23*(4).

Donaldson, L. (1990). The Ethereal Hand: Organizational Economics and Management Theory. *Academy of Management Review, 15*(3), 369–381.

Dossena, G. (2010). *Entrepreneurship Today.* McGraw-Hill.

Eagly, A. H., & Carli, L. L. (2003). The Female Leadership Advantage: An Evaluation of the Evidence. *The Leadership Quarterly, 14*(6), 807–34.

Ees, H., Gabrielsson, J. & Huse, M. (2009). Toward a Behavioral Theory of Boards and Corporate Governance. *Corporate Governance: An International Review, 17*(3), 307–19.

Fama, E. F. (1980). Agency Problems and the Theory of the Firm. *Journal of Political Economy, 88*(2), 288–307.

Fama, E. F., & Jensen, M. C. (1983a). Separation of Ownership and Control. *The Journal of Law and Economics, 26*(2), 301–25.

Fama, E. F., & Jensen, M. C. (1983b). Agency Problems and Residual Claims. *The Journal of Law and Economics, 26*(2), 327–49.

Felin, T., Foss, N. J. & Ployhart, R. E. (2015). The Microfoundations Movement in Strategy and Organization Theory. *The Academy of Management Annals, 9*(1), 575–632.

Filatotchev, I., Strange, R., Piesse, J. & Lien, Y. C. (2007). FDI by Firms from newly Industrialised Economies in Emerging Markets: Corporate Governance, Entry Mode and Location. *Journal of International Business Studies, 38*(4), 556–72.

Finegold, D., Benson, G. S. & Hecht, D. (2007). Corporate Boards and Company Performance: Review of Research in Light of Recent Reforms. *Corporate Governance: An International Review, 15*(5), 865–78.

Finkelstein, S., & Mooney, A. C. (2003). Not the Usual Suspects: How to Use Board Process to Make Boards Better. *The Academy of Management Executive, 17*(2), 101–13.

Forbes, D. P., & Milliken, F. J. (1999). Cognition and Corporate Governance: Understanding Boards of Directors as Strategic Decision-making Groups. *Academy of Management Review, 24*(3), 489–505.

Foss, N. J., Husted, K. & Michailova, S. (2010). Governing Knowledge Sharing in Organizations: Levels of Analysis, Governance Mechanisms, and Research Directions. *Journal of Management Studies, 47*(3), 455–82.

Foss, N. J., & Lindenberg, S. (2013). Microfoundations for Strategy: A Goal-framing Perspective on the Drivers of Value Creation. *The Academy of Management Perspectives, 27*(2), 85–102.

Gabrielsson, J., Calabrò, A. & Huse, M. (2016). Boards and Value Creation in Family Firms: An Extended Team Production Approach. In R. Leblanc (ed.), *The Handbook of Board Governance: A Comprehensive Guide for Public, Private and Not-for-Profit Board Members*. Wiley, 748–63.

Gabrielsson, J., Calabrò, A., Ees, H., Minichilli, A. & Zattoni, A. (2014) Editorial. *International Journal of Business Governance and Ethics, 9*(2), 115–20.

Gabrielsson, J., & Huse, M. (2004). Context, Behavior, and Evolution: Challenges in Research on Boards and Governance. *International Studies of Management & Organization, 34*(2), 11–36.

Gabrielsson, J., & Huse, M. (2009). Boards of Directors and Corporate Innovation. In G. Dossena (ed.), *Entrepreneurs and Entrepreneurship.* McGrawHill, Chap. 13.

Gabrielsson, J., Huse, M. & Minichilli, A. (2007). Understanding the Leadership Role of the Board Chairperson through a Team Production Approach. *International Journal of Leadership Studies, 3*(1), 21–39.

Gill, R., & Scharff, C. (eds.). (2013). *New Femininities: Postfeminism, Neoliberalism and Subjectivity.* Springer.

Goldeng, E. (2017). Powerful Women on Boards: Sources of Power among Boards of Directors and the Effect on the Gender of the new CEO. Presentation EGOS Copenhagen.

Ghoshal, S. (2005). Bad Management Theories Are Destroying Good Management Practices. *Academy of Management Learning & Education, 4*(1), 75–91.

Grandori, A. (2004). *Corporate Governance and Firm Organization: Microfoundations and Structural Forms.* Oxford University Press.

Grant, R. M. (1996). Toward a Knowledge-based Theory of the Firm. *Strategic Management Journal, 17*(S2), 109–22.

Grosvold, J., & Brammer, S. (2011). National Institutional Systems as Antecedents of Female Board Representation: An Empirical Study. *Corporate Governance: An International Review, 19*(2), 116–35.

Hakim, C. (2000). *Work-lifestyle Choices in the 21st Century: Preference Theory.* Oxford University Press.

Hakim, C. (2011). *Erotic Capital: The Power of Attraction in the Boardroom and the Bedroom.* Basic Books.

Hambrick, D. C., Werder, A. V. & Zajac, E. J. (2008). New Directions in Corporate Governance Research. *Organization Science, 19*(3), 381–85.

Hamel, G., & Prahalad, C. K. (1990). Corporate Imagination and Expeditionary Marketing. *Harvard Business Review, 69*(4), 81–92.

Hansen, K., & Huse, M. (2011). Erfahrungen aus Norwegen: Nutzbar für Deutschland. In Deutsche Juristinnenverband *Aktionärinnen Fordern Gleichberechtigung*, Bundesministerium für Familie, Senioren und Jugend, 117–21.

House, R., Hanges, J., Javidan, M., Dorfman, P. W., & Gupta, V. (2004). *Culture, Leadership and Organizations: The GLOBE Study of 62 Societies.* Sage.

Huse, M. (1993). Relational Norms as a Supplement to Neo-classical Understanding of Directorates: An Empirical Study of Boards of Directors. *Journal of Socio-Economics, 22*(3), 219–40.

Huse, M. (1994a). *Distansert Nærhet: en studie om Betydningen av Relasjonene mellom Styre og Ledelse for Faktisk Styreatferd.* PhD thesis Nordland Research Institute.

Huse, M. (1994b). Board-Management Relations in Small Firms: The Paradox of Simultaneous Independence and Interdependence. *Small Business Economics Journal, 6*(1), 55–72.

Huse, M. (1998). Researching the Dynamics of Board—Stakeholder Relations. *Long Range Planning, 31*(2), 218–26.

Huse, M. (2000). A Way Forward: Programs to Increase the Number of Women on Boards. Presentation at the Academy of Management, Washington DC.

Huse, M. (2005). Accountability and Creating Accountability: A Framework for Exploring Behavioural Perspectives of Corporate Governance. *British Journal of Management, 16*, s65–80.

Huse, M. (2007). *Boards, Governance and Value Creation: The Human Side of Corporate Governance.* Cambridge University Press.

Huse, M. (ed.). (2009a). *The Value Creating Board: Corporate Governance and Organizational Behaviour.* Routledge.

Huse, M. (2009b). Building Blocks in Understanding Behaviourial Perspectives of Boards: Developing a Research Stream. In Huse, M. (ed.), *The Value Creating Board: Corporate Governance and Organizational Behaviour* Routledge, 57–69.

Huse, M. (2009c). The Value Creating Boards Surveys: A Benchmark. In Huse, M. (ed.), *The Value Creating Board: Corporate Governance and Organizational Behaviour.* Routledge, 367–84.

Huse, M. (2010). Kvinner i Styret: Lærdommer fra Norge. *Magma, 13*(7), 46–55.

Huse, M. (2011a). The Golden Skirts: Changes in Board Composition following Gender Quotas on Corporate Boards. Presentation at Australian and New Zealand Academy Meeting, Wellington, NZ.

Huse, M. (2011b). *Styret: Tante, Barbar eller Klan.* Fagbokforlaget.

Huse, M. (2012). The Golden Skirts: Lessons from Norway about Women on Corporate Boards. In S. Gröschl & J. Takagi (eds.) *Diversity Quotas, Diverse Perspective: The Case of Genders.* Glower/Ashgate, Chap. 1.

Huse, M. (2013). Has the Law Been a Success? Presentation at the House of Commons. In J. Edmonds & E. Tutchell (eds.), *Made in Norway: How Norwegians Have Used Quotas to Increase the Number of Women on Company Boards.* Fabian Society and the Labour Finance and Industry Group, Chap. 5.

Huse, M. (2014). Norway: The Norwegian Gender Balance Law – a Benchmark? In M. De Vos & P. Culliford (ed.), *Gender Quotas in the Boards of Directors*. Intersentia, Chap. 10.

Huse, M. (2016). Getting Women on Boards: Norwegian Experiences and the International Landscape. March 8th Speech Slovenian National Council.

Huse, M. (2018). Gender in the Boardroom: Learnings from World-Leader Norway. *FACTBase Bulletin 58*, The University of Western Australia and the Committee of Perth, Perth.

Huse, M., & Gabrielsson, J. (2012). Board Leadership and Value Creation: An Extended Team Production approach. *The SAGE Handbook of Corporate Governance*. Sage, Chap,11.

Huse, M., Gabrielsson, J. & Minichilli, A. (2009a). How Boards Contribute to Value Creation. In M. Huse (ed.) *The Value Creating Board: Corporate Governance and Organisational Behaviour*, Routledge, Chap. 28.

Huse, M., Gabrielsson, J. & Minichilli, A. (2009b). Improving Corporate Governance Practices. In R. Burke & C. Cooper (eds.) *Peak Performing Organizations*. Routledge, Chap. 16.

Huse, M., Göke, J., Möltner, H. & Rigolini, A. (2017) 'Lean in' and Variations in Gender Discourses about Getting Women on Boards. Presentation at EGOS meeting, Copenhagen.

Huse, M., Hoskisson, R., Zattoni, A. & Viganò, R. (2011). New Perspectives on Board Research: Changing the Research Agenda. *Journal of Management & Governance*, *15*(1), 5–28.

Huse, M., Nielsen, S. T. & Hagen, I. M. (2009) Women and Employee-Elected Board Members, and Their Contributions to Board Control Tasks. *Journal of Business Ethics*, *89*(4), 581–97.

Huse, M., & Grethe Solberg, A. (2006). Gender-related Boardroom Dynamics: How Scandinavian Women Make and Can Make Contributions on Corporate Boards. *Women in Management Review*, *21*(2), 113–30.

Huse, M., & Søland, A. I. (2009). *Styreledelse: Styret som Team og Prosessorientert Styrearbeid*. Fagbokforlaget.

Iannotta, M., Gatti, M. & Huse, M. (2016). Institutional Complementarities and Gender Diversity on Boards: A Configurational Approach. *Corporate Governance: An International Review*, *24*(4), 406–27.

Izquierdo, M., Huse, M., & Möltner, H. (2016). *Value Creating Boards and Gender Diversity: Suggestions to Progress in Getting Women on Boards in Spain*. BI Norwegian Business School.

Jensen, M. C., & Meckling, W. H. (1976). Theory of the Firm: Managerial Behavior, Agency Costs and Ownership Structure. *Journal of Financial Economics, 3*(4), 305–60.

Jensen, M. C., & Ruback, R. S. (1983). The Market for Corporate Control: The Scientific Evidence. *Journal of Financial Economics, 11*(1–4), 5–50.

Johnson, J. L., Daily, C. M. & Ellstrand, A. E. (1996). Boards of Directors: A Review and Research Agenda. *Journal of Management, 22*(3), 409–38.

Johnson, S. G., Schnatterly, K. & Hill, A. D. (2013). Board Composition beyond Independence: Social Capital, Human Capital, and Demographics. *Journal of Management, 39*(1), 232–62.

Judge, W. Q., & Talaulicar, T. (2017). Board Involvement in the Strategic Decision Making Process: A Comprehensive Review. *Annals of Corporate Governance, 2*(2), 51–169.

Kanadlı, S. B., Torchia, M. & Gabaldon, P. (2017). Increasing Women's Contribution on Board Decision Making: The Importance of Chairperson Leadership Efficacy and Board Openness. *European Management Journal.* Online 27. March.

Kang, H., Cheng, M. & Gray, S. J. (2007). Corporate Governance and Board Composition: Diversity and Independence of Australian Boards. *Corporate Governance: An International Review, 15*(2), 194–207.

Kanter, R. M. (1976). The Impact of Hierarchical Structures on the Work Behavior of Women and Men. *Social Problems, 23*(4), 415–30.

Kaufman, A., & Englander, E. (2005). A Team Production Model of Corporate Governance. *The Academy of Management Executive, 19*(3), 9–22.

Kehoe, C., Lund, F. & Spielmann, N. (2016). Toward a Value-creating Board. Downloaded February 2017 from McKinsey & Company: www.mckinsey.com/business-functions/strategy-and-corporate-finance/our-insights/toward-a-value-creating-board.

Kirsch, A. (2017). The Gender Composition of Corporate Boards: A Review and Research Agenda. *Leadership Quarterly.* Online 20. June.

Kosnik, R. D. (1987). Greenmail: A study of Board Performance in Corporate Governance. *Administrative Science Quarterly, 32*, 163–85.

Lizardo, O. (2004). The Cognitive Origins of Bourdieu's Habitus. *Journal for the Theory of Social Behaviour, 34*(4), 375–401.

Mace, M. L. (1971). *Directors: Myth and Reality.* Harvard Business School Press

Machold, S., Huse, M., Hansen, K. & Brogi, M. (eds.). (2013). *Getting Women on to Corporate Boards: A Snowball Starting in Norway.* Edward Elgar Publishing.

Machold, S., Huse, M., Minichilli, A. & Nordqvist, M. (2011). Board Leadership and Strategy Involvement in Small Firms: A Team Production Approach. *Corporate Governance: An International Review*, *19*(4), 368–83.

Mallin, C. A. (ed.). (2011). *Handbook on International Corporate Governance: Country Analyses*. Edward Elgar Publishing.

March, J. G., & Simon, H. A. (1958). *Organizations*. Wiley.

Marcus, G. E. (2016). Multi-sited Ethnography: Notes and Queries. In Falzon, M-A. (ed.), *Multi-sited Ethnography: Theory, Praxis, and Locality in Contemporary Research*. Routledge, Chap. 10.

Melkumov, D., Breit, E. & Khoreva, V. (2015). Directors' Social Identifications and Board Tasks: Evidence from Finland. *Corporate Governance: An International Review*, *23*(1), 42–59.

Minichilli, A., Zattoni, A. & Zona, F. (2009). Making Boards Effective: An Empirical E xamination of Board Task Performance. *British Journal of Management*, *20*(1), 55–74.

Minichilli, A., Zattoni, A., Nielsen, S. & Huse, M. (2012). Board Task Performance: An Exploration of Micro- and Macro-level Determinants of Board Effectiveness. *Journal of Organizational Behavior*, *33*(2), 193–215.

Möltner, H., Huse, M. & Göke, J. 2017. Women's Motivation Matters: A Review on Women and Leadership. Presentation at EAWOP Conference, Dublin, May.

Monks, R., & Minow, N. (1995). *Corporate Governance*. Blackwell.

Nadler, D. A., (2004). What is the Board's Role in Strategy Development? Engaging the Board in Corporate Corporate Strategy, *Strategy & Leadership*, 32(5) 25–33 .

Nielsen, S. T., & Huse, M. (2010a). Women Director's Contribution to Board Decision-making and Strategic Involvement: The Role of Equality Perceptions. *European Management Review*, *7*, 16–29.

Nielsen, S. T., & Huse, M. (2010b). The Contribution of Women on Boards of Directors: Going beyond the Surface. *Corporate Governance: An International Review*, *18*(2): 136–48.

Nielsen, S. T., & Huse, M. (2012). How Do Women Directors Make a Difference to the Work of Corporate Boards: Evidence from Norway. In R. Nielsen & C. D. Tvarmø (eds.) *Scandinavian Women's Law in the 21st Century*, Jurist og Økonomiforbundets Forlag, Chap. 10.

Ogburn, W. F. (1922). *Social Change with Respect to Culture and Original Nature*. BW Huebsch.

Oshry, B., Hermalin, B. E. & Weisbach, M. S. (2010). The Role of Boards of Directors in Corporate Governance: A Conceptual Framework and Survey. *Journal of Economic Literature, 48*(1), 58–107.

Osterloh, M., & Frey, B. S. (2000). Motivation, Knowledge Transfer, and Organizational Forms. *Organization Science, 11*(5), 538–50.

Osterloh, M., Frey, B. S. & Frost, J. (2001). Managing Motivation, Organization and Governance. *Journal of Management and Governance, 5*(3), 231–39.

Oxelheim, L., Gregorič, A., Randøy, T. & Thomsen, S. (2013). On the Internationalization of Corporate Boards: The Case of Nordic Firms. *Journal of International Business Studies, 44*(3), 173–94.

Petrovic, J. (2008). Unlocking the Role of a Board Director: A Review of the Literature. *Management Decision, 46*(9), 1373–92.

Pettigrew, A. M. (1992). On Studying Managerial Elites. *Strategic Management Journal, 13*(S2), 163–82.

Pettigrew, A. M. (1997). What Is a Processual Analysis? *Scandinavian Journal of Management, 13*(4), 337–48.

Pierce, C. (2016). Trends in Corporate Governance. In R. Leblanc (ed.), *Handbook of Board Governance.* Wiley, Chap. 3.

Porter, M. (1995). *Competitive Advantage: Creating and Sustaining Competitive Advantage.* Press Ganey Associates.

Porter, M., & Kramer, M. R. (2011). Creating Shared Value: How to Reinvent Capitalism – and Unleash a Wave of Innovation and Growth. *Harvard Business Review*, January-February, 1–17.

Post, C., & Byron, K. (2015). Women on Boards and Firm Financial Performance: A Meta-analysis. *Academy of Management Journal, 58*(5), 1546–71.

Pugliese, A., Bezemer, P. J., Zattoni, A., Huse, M., Van den Bosch, F. A. & Volberda, H. W. (2009). Boards of Directors' Contribution to Strategy: A Literature Review and Research Agenda. *Corporate Governance: An International Review, 17*(3), 292–306.

Pye, A., & Pettigrew, A. (2005). Studying Board Context, Process and Dynamics: Some Challenges for the Future. *British Journal of Management, 16*(s1), 27–38.

Reich, R. (2013). *Inequality for all,* www.imdb.com/title/tt2215151/ (downloaded May 14, 2017).

Rennison, B. W. (2012). *Knæk Kønnets Koder: Kvinder i Ledelse.* Gyldendal Business.

Rigolini, A., Huse, M. & Göke, J. (2017). Who Are the Women Being Appointed to Boards: The Effects of Tokenism and Quotas. Presentation at the Italian Academy of Management (AIDEA), September.

Schønning, A. (2013). *Investigating Absorptive Capacity in Boards: Corporate Governance and Value Creating Boards.* PhD thesis, Wolverhampton University.

Sealy, R., & Vinnicombe, S. (2012). The Female FTSE Board Report 2012: Milestone or Millstone? Cranfield International Centre for Women Leaders.

Seierstad, C., Gabaldon, P., Groeschl, S. & Huse, M. (2016). Women in Norway: The Multiple Paths to Boards. Presentation at the Academy of Management Meeting, Anaheim, August.

Seierstad, C., & Opsahl, T. (2011). For the Few not for the Many: The Effects of Affirmative Action on Presence, Prominence and Social Capital of Women Directors in Norway. *Scandinavian Journal of Management, 27*(1): 44–54.

Seierstad, C., Warner-Søderholm, G., Torchia, M. & Huse, M. (2017). Increasing the Number of Women on Boards: The Role of Actors and Processes. *Journal of Business Ethics, 141*(2), 289–315.

Sellevoll, T., Huse, M., & Hansen, C. (2007). *The Value Creating Board. Results from the 'Follow-Up Surveys' 2005/2006 in Norwegian Firms.* BI Norwegian Business School.

Teece, D. J., Pisano, G. & Shuen, A. (1997). Dynamic Capabilities and Strategic Management. *Strategic Management Journal, 18*(7), 509–33.

Teigen, M. (2012). Gender Quotas on Corporate Boards: On the Diffusion of a Distinct National Policy Reform. In F. Engelstad (ed.), *Firms, Boards and Gender Quotas: Comparative Perspectives.* Emerald Group Publishing Limited, Chap. 4.

Terjesen, S., Aguilera, R. V. & Lorenz, R. (2015). Legislating a Woman's Seat on the Board: Institutional Factors Driving Gender Quotas for Boards of Directors. *Journal of Business Ethics, 128*(2), 233–51.

Terjesen, S., Sealy, R. & Singh, V. (2009). Women Directors on Corporate Boards: A Review and Research Agenda. *Corporate Governance: An International Review, 17*(3), 320–37.

Thomsen, S. (2008). A Minimum Theory of Boards. *International Journal of Corporate Governance, 1*(1): 73–96

Thomsen, S., & Pedersen, T. (2000). Ownership Structure and Economic Performance in the Largest European Companies. *Strategic Management Journal, 21*(6), 689–705.

Torchia, M., Calabrò, A. & Huse, M. (2011). Women Directors on Corporate Boards: From Tokenism to Critical Mass. *Journal of Business Ethics, 102*(2), 299-317.

Tørlen, T. (2015). *Changes among Women Directors with Multiple Directorships - a Longitudinal Study of the Women Board Elite.* Master's thesis in Strategy, BI Norwegian Business School.

De Vos, M., & Culliford, P. (eds.). (2014). *Gender Quotas for Company Boards*. Intersentia.

Warner-Søderholm, G., Bertsch, A., Seierstad, C. & Huse, M. (2017) Getting Women on Boards: What Matters? Paper presented at the Nordic Academy of Management, Reykjavik

Wellalage, N. H., & Locke, S. (2013). Women on Board, Firm Financial Performance and Agency Costs. *Asian Journal of Business Ethics, 2*(2), 113-27.

Wenstøp, P. Z. (2008). *Effective Board Task Performance: Searching for Understanding into Board Failure and Success.* PhD thesis, BI Norwegian Business School.

Westphal, J. D., & Zajac, E. J. (2013). A Behavioral Theory of Corporate Governance: Explicating the Mechanisms of Socially Situated and Socially Constituted Agency. *Academy of Management Annals, 7*(1), 607-61.

Williams, J. C., & Segal, N. (2003). Beyond the Maternal Wall: Relief for Family Caregivers Who Are Discriminated against on the Job. *Harvard Women's Law Journal, 26*, 77-162.

Wright, M., Filatotchev, I., Hoskisson, R. E. & Peng, M. W. (2005). Strategy Research in Emerging Economies: Challenging the Conventional Wisdom. *Journal of Management Studies, 42*(1), 1-33.

Young, M. N., Peng, M. W., Ahlstrom, D., Bruton, G. D. & Jiang, Y. (2008). Corporate Governance in Emerging Economies: A Review of the Principal-Principal Perspective. *Journal of Management Studies, 45*(1), 196-220.

Zahra, S. A., & George, G. (2002). Absorptive Capacity: A Review, Reconceptualization, and Extension. *Academy of Management Review, 27*(2), 185-203.

Zahra, S. A., & Pearce, J. A. (1989). Boards of Directors and Corporate Financial Performance: A Review and Integrative Model. *Journal of Management, 15*(2), 291-334.

Zattoni, A., Gnan, L., & Huse, M. (2015). Does Family Involvement Influence Firm Performance? Exploring the Mediating Effects of Board Processes and Tasks. *Journal of Management, 41*(4), 1214–43.

Zhang, P. (2010). Board Information and Strategic Tasks Performance. *Corporate Governance: An International Review, 18*(5), 473–87.

Zona, F., & Zattoni, A. (2007). Beyond the Black Box of Demography: Board Processes and Task Effectiveness within Italian Firms. *Corporate Governance: An International Review, 15*(5), 852–64.

Cambridge Elements ☰

Corporate Governance

Thomas Clarke

UTS Business School, University of Technology Sydney
Thomas Clarke is Professor of Corporate Governance at the UTS Business School of the University of Technology Sydney. His work focuses on the institutional diversity of corporate governance and his most recent book is *International Corporate Governance* (Second Edition 2017). He is interested in questions about the purposes of the corporation, and the convergence of the concerns of corporate governance and corporate sustainability.

About the series

The series Elements in Corporate Governance focuses on the significant emerging field of corporate governance. Authoritative, lively and compelling analyses include expert surveys of the foundations of the discipline, original insights into controversial debates, frontier developments, and masterclasses on key issues. Its areas of interest include empirical studies of corporate governance in practice, regional institutional diversity, emerging fields, key problems and core theoretical perspectives.

Cambridge Elements ≡
Corporate Governance

Elements in the series

Asian Corporate Governance: Trends and Challenges
Toru Yoshikawa

Value-Creating Boards: Challenges for Future Practice and Research
Morten Huse

A full series listing is available at: www.cambridge.org/ECG

Printed in the United States
By Bookmasters